SPMG

HEINEM MATHEMATICS

Textbook

These are the different types of pages and symbols used in this book and associated workbooks.

1
Mental addition of single digits

Most textbook and workbook pages are of this type. They deal with mathematical concepts, skills and applications in number, measure, shape and handling data.

17
Other activity: addition, multiplication

These pages provide self-contained activities which need not necessarily be tackled in the order in which they are presented. They are intended to give further opportunities for children to apply the mathematics they have learned or to extend their experience.

Problem solving

Some pages, or parts of a page, provide an opportunity for problem solving or investigative work.

Where a calculator would be useful this is indicated by a calculator symbol.

R 25

This symbol indicates that more work of this kind can be found on the numbered Reinforcement Sheet.

Heinemann Educational,
a Division of Heinemann Publishers (Oxford) Ltd,
Halley Court, Jordan Hill, Oxford OX2 8EJ

First Published 1994 ISBN 0 435 02190 7

Photographs by Chris Coggins, with the help of staff and pupils at Botley County Primary School, Oxford.

Designed by Miller, Craig and Cocking
Produced by Oxprint
Printed in the UK by Bath Colour Books, Glasgow

98 97 96 95 94

10 9 8 7 6 5 4 3 2 1

Heinemann

Contents

Measure		Textbook	Workbook	Reinf't Sheets	Extension Textbook
Length	Measuring to nearest metre: perimeter	67, 68			
	Measuring to nearest centimetre: perimeter	69	16		
	Addition and subtraction	70		25	
	Tenths of a metre	71			
Area	Square centimetres; irregular shapes	72	27, 28		E14, 15
	Square metres	73, 74			
Weight	20g, 10g, 5g weights	75, 76			
	Reading scales	77–9	29	26, 27	
	Addition and subtraction		30		
Time	Clocks: times to the nearest minute, am/pm	80–84			
	Durations	85–8	7	28, 29	E16, 17
	Calendars and dates	89, 90			
Volume	Quarter litres	92			
	Cubic centimetres	93, 94			E19
Measure	Scales and problems		31–3		
Other activity		91			

Shape					
Symmetry	Lines of symmetry: one, two, more than two	95–7	17, 18		E20
Tiling	Making and drawing tilings		24–6		
3D shape	Nets and skeleton solids: cubes, cuboids	99–101			E22
Angles	Comparing angles		20–22		
	Degrees; turning, compass directions	103–4		30	E24, 25
	Movement and pathways	105–6	23		
Grid references	Using grid references	107–8			

Handling data					
Handling data	Bar graphs	111–14			
	Grouped tallies, surveys, tables	115–18	34–6		E28–30
	Averages	119–21			
Probability	Likelihood	122–3			
Other activities		98, 102, 109 110, 124, 125			E1, 7, 21
Record of Work grids			37–9		

Kelvin, Kate, Lisa and Tony use an old chart to explore a cave.

1 Add mentally. Write the answers.

(a) 8 + 6 + 5 (b) 3 + 7 + 5 + 3 (c) 6 + 8 + 4 + 2

(d) 5 + 9 + 5 + 6

(e) 9, 8, +, 3, 2

(f) 7, 6, 9, 4, +

(g) 6, 7, 3, 5, 6, +

(h) +, 5, 8, 9, 9

(i) 6 + 6, 4, 6, 6

(j) 5, 5, 4, 5, 4

(k) 1, 2 3, 4 5 6

Problem solving

1	2	3	4	5	6	7	8	9	10	11	12	13	14	15	16

2 Find **four** numbers, next to each other, which add to give **30**.

3 Make each total from 11 to 20 using only **3**s and **5**s.

Hint ⇨ 3 + 5 + 5 = 13

In the tunnel . . .

Use the code and your answers to find the message which opens the door.

Add mentally. Write the answers.

1 (a) 52 + 4 (b) 43 + 5 (c) 82 + 2 (d) 4 + 71
(e) 42 + 10 (f) 42 + 9 (g) 38 + 10 (h) 38 + 9
(i) 25 + 9 (j) 10 + 53 (k) 37 + 9 (l) 41 + 10

76 + 7 is the same as 70 + 6 + 7
= 70 + 13 = 83

2 (a) 38 + 8 (b) 68 + 7 (c) 49 + 7 (d) 57 + 6
(e) 37 + 7 (f) 38 + 4 (g) 45 + 6 (h) 89 + 3
(i) 6 + 36 (j) 46 + 7 (k) 27 + 8 (l) 58 + 5
(m) 56 + 8 (n) 78 + 8 (o) 47 + 9 (p) 87 + 5

3 Write the missing numbers.
(a) 24 + ☐ = 30 (b) 56 + ☐ = 60 (c) 33 + ☐ = 40
(d) 75 + ☐ = 80 (e) 89 + ☐ = 90 (f) 48 + ☐ = 50

76 + 7 is the same as 76 + 4 + 3
= 80 + 3 = 83

4 Add mentally. Write the answers.
(a) 57 + 5 (b) 55 + 8 (c) 64 + 7 (d) 89 + 8
(e) 48 + 8 (f) 84 + 8 (g) 69 + 6 (h) 55 + 7
(i) 66 + 9 (j) 56 + 7 (k) 67 + 8 (l) 54 + 8

5 Write the complete message.

Code	
1	I
2	X
4	W
5	S
6	T
7	O
34	D
35	W
42	C
44	–
46	A
47	E
48	U
51	L
52	B
53	K
56	T
62	E
63	I
64	S
71	G
75	N
84	R
86	E
92	O
97	H

Go to Workbook page 1.

The treasure trail

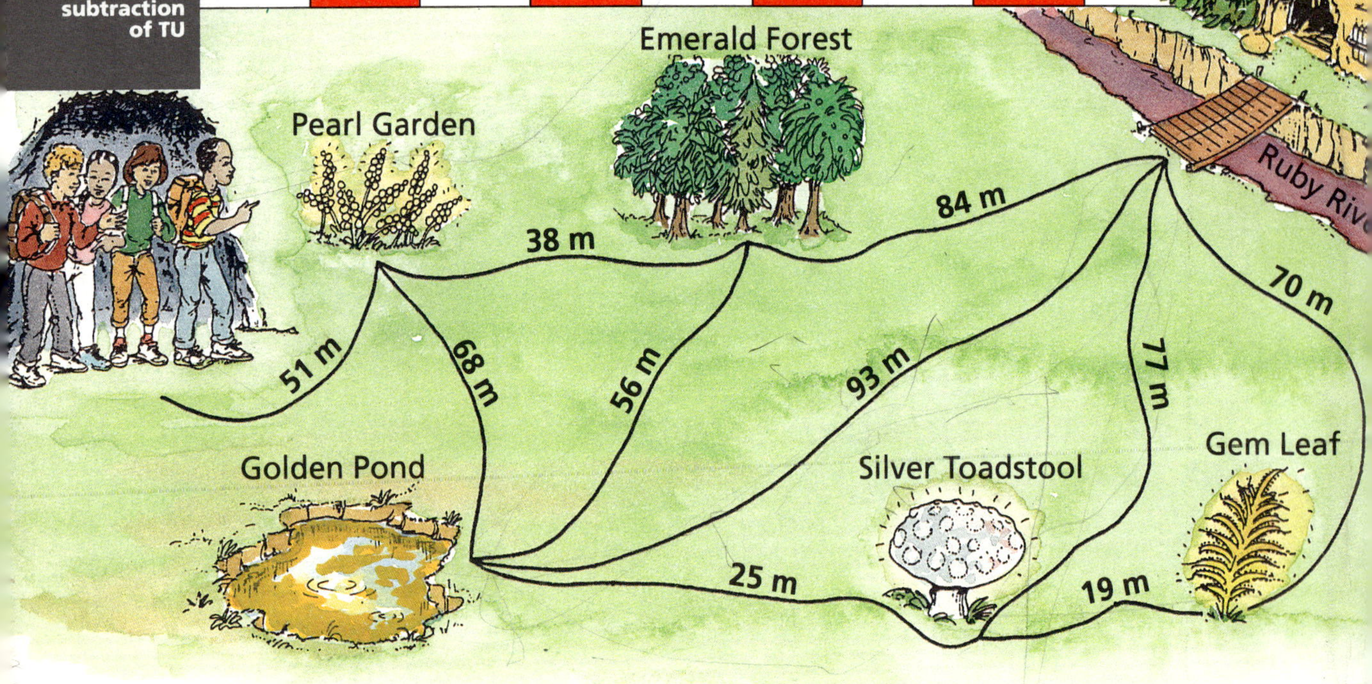

The children explore the treasure trail.

1 Find the total distance in metres for each journey.

(a) The Cave ⟶ Pearl Garden ⟶ Emerald Forest

(b) Golden Pond ⟶ Silver Toadstool ⟶ Ruby River

(c) Pearl Garden ⟶ Golden Pond ⟶ Ruby River

(d) Emerald Forest ⟶ Golden Pond ⟶ Ruby River

2 Make up four other journeys like these and write the total distance for each.

3 (a) Use **both** maps. Find how far each child still has to walk to reach Ruby River.

(b) Who has furthest to go? How much further is it than for each of the others?

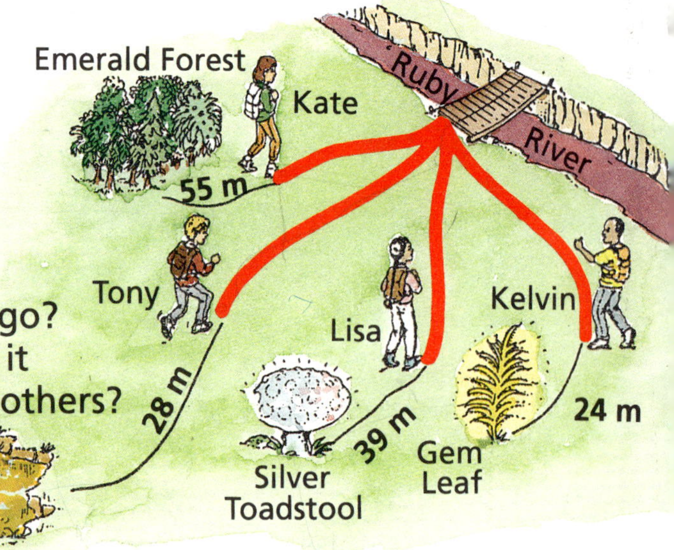

Problem solving

4 The owl flew 102 m along two paths to Ruby River.

(a) Where did it start?

(b) What did it pass on the way?

Crossing Ruby River

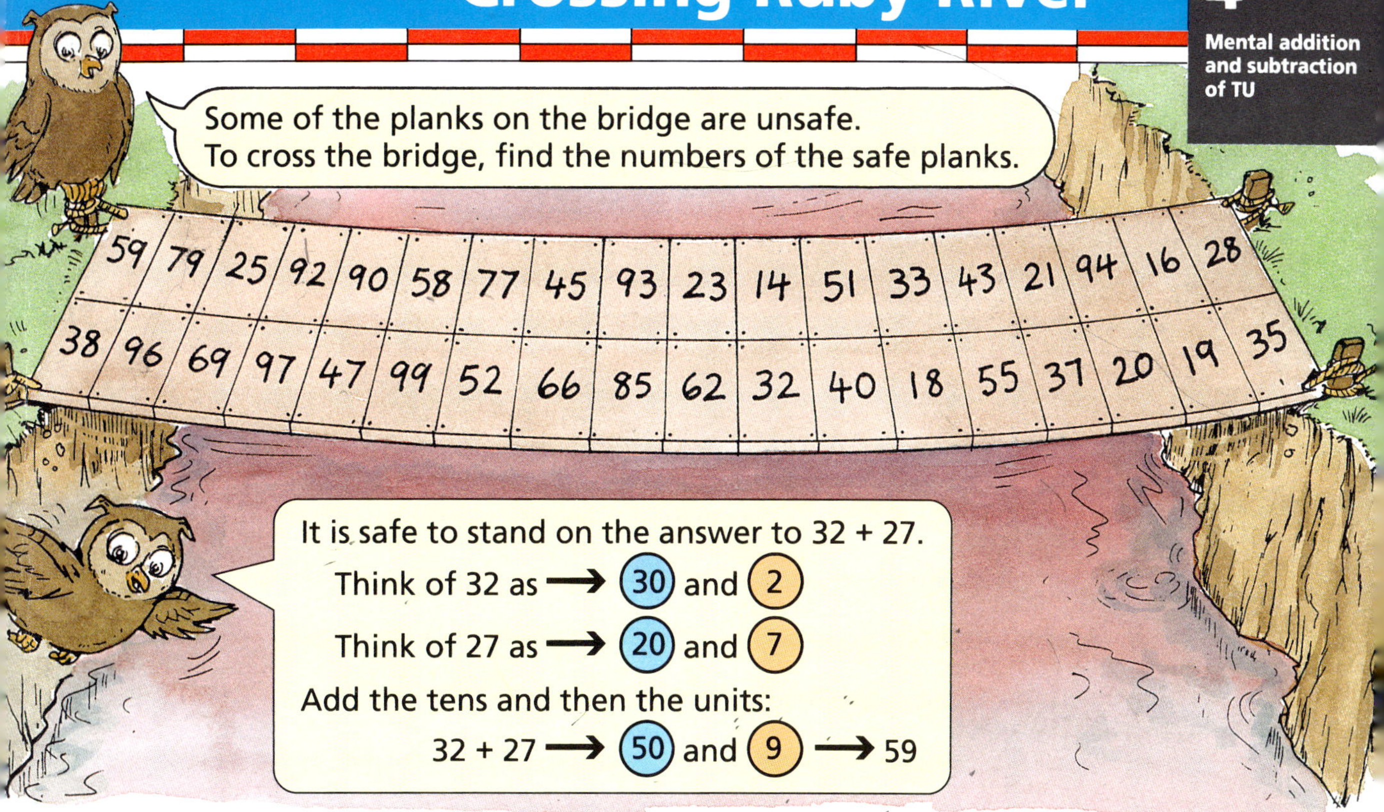

1 Add to find safe numbers.

(a) 33 + 46	**(b)** 21 + 75	**(c)** 53 + 16	**(d)** 12 + 80
(e) 55 + 42	**(f)** 31 + 16	**(g)** 21 + 37	**(h)** 33 + 66
(i) 43 + 34	**(j)** 21 + 24	**(k)** 32 + 34	**(l)** 40 + 45

It is safe to stand on the answer to 58 − 35.

Think of 58 as → 50 and 8

Think of 35 as → 30 and 5

Subtract the tens and then the units:

58 − 35 → 20 and 3 → 23

2 Subtract to find safe numbers.

(a) 99 − 37	**(b)** 86 − 72	**(c)** 45 − 13	**(d)** 78 − 27
(e) 78 − 60	**(f)** 67 − 34	**(g)** 64 − 21	**(h)** 72 − 51
(i) 69 − 32	**(j)** 66 − 46	**(k)** 38 − 22	**(l)** 89 − 61

3 Make up your own additions or subtractions for these safe numbers.

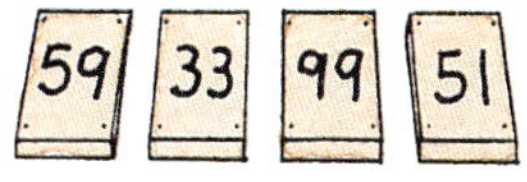

4 Which are the unsafe numbers on the bridge?

5 Addition and subtraction of HTU

The Pyramid

1 Find the answers and I will light the candles.

(a) 432 + 158

(b) 167 + 258

(c) 309 + 96

(d) 369 + 275

2 Copy and complete.

(a) 326 − 134
(b) 287 − 93
(c) 580 − 271
(d) 403 − 115
(e) 300 − 128

(f) 601 − 218
(g) 326 − 158
(h) 285 − 109
(i) 600 − 123

(j) 404 − 128
(k) 200 − 86
(l) 417 − 178

Problem solving

3 Look at the pattern of answers in question 2. How should Lisa set the levers?

4 (a) Find the answers.

(b) Make up **two** more examples to continue the pattern of the answers.

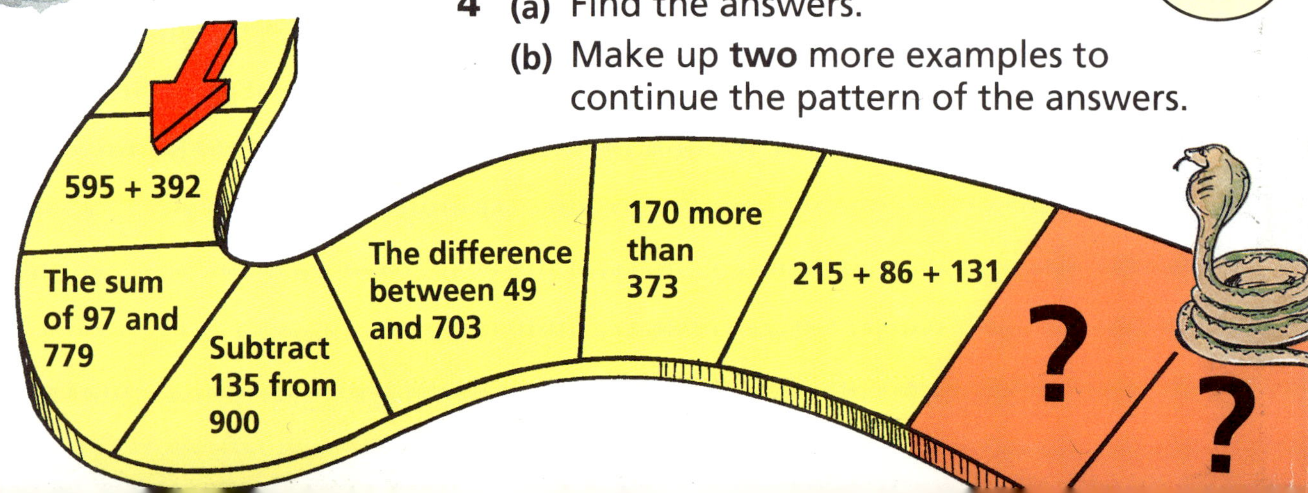

The treasure

6 Addition and subtraction of HTU

1 Find the answers for each path. (Each answer follows on from the one before.)

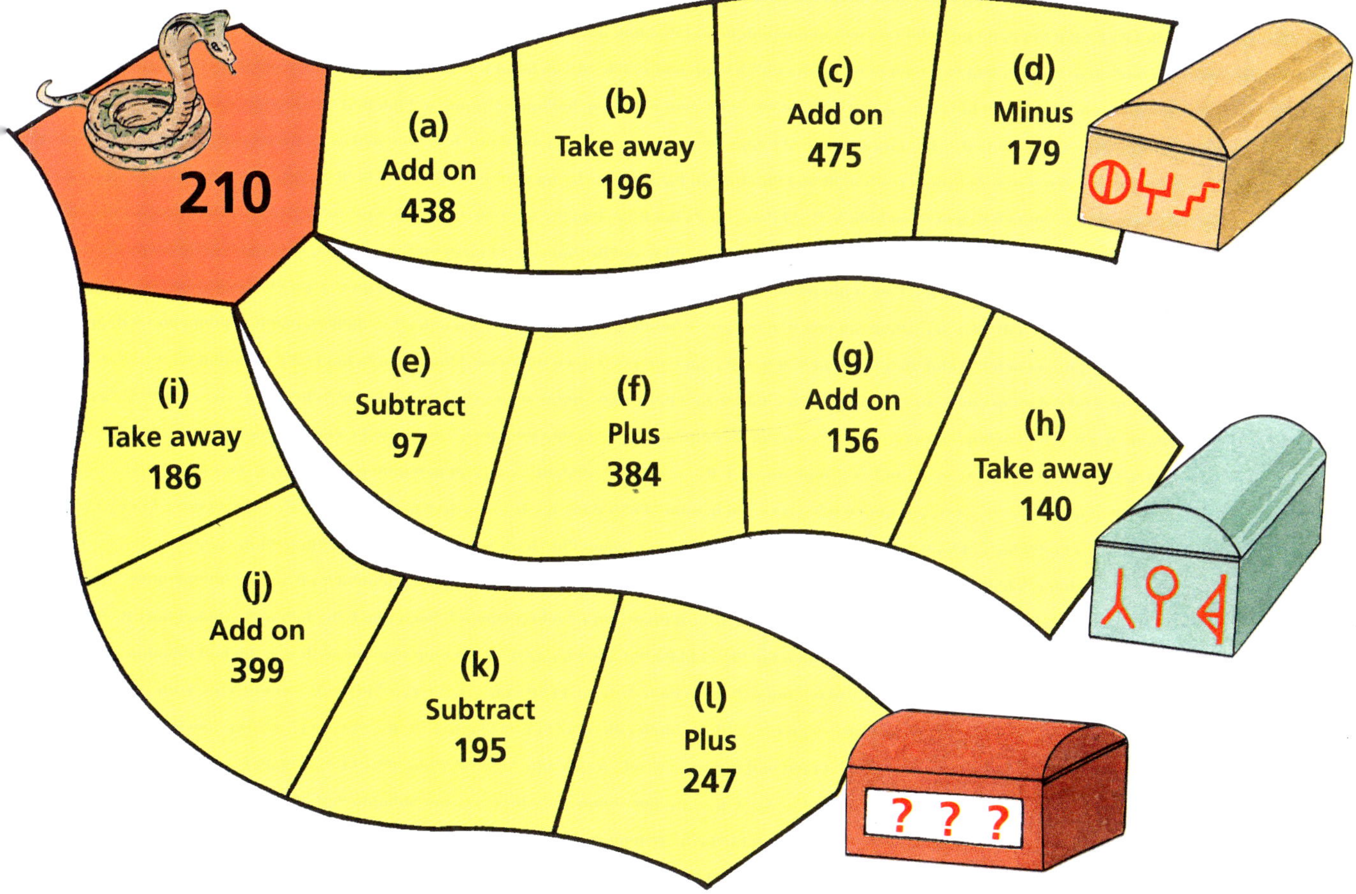

2 Which symbols should be written on the red box?

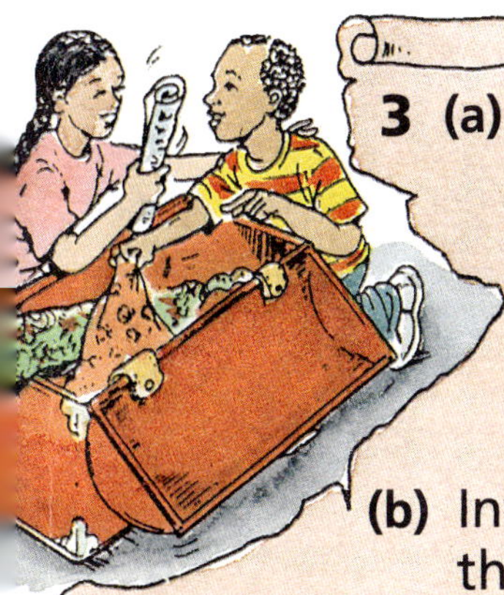

3 (a)
- Choose a two-digit number.
- Reverse the digits to make a second number.
- Find the difference between the two numbers.
- Do this for other two-digit numbers.
- What do you notice about **the sum of the digits** in each of your answers?

Problem solving

(b) Investigate what happens when you try this with three-digit numbers.
Look at the signpost. The explorers must follow the sign that matches your answer. Where will they go next?

Go to Workbook page 2.

Tree puzzles

1 Copy and complete these sequences.

(a) 600, 700, 800, ____, ____, ____

(b) 6400, 6300, 6200, ____, ____, ____

(c) 500, 1000, 1500, ____, ____, ____

(d) 2000, 1950, 1900, ____, ____, ____

2 Put these numbers in order, starting with the smallest.

3 Use all four digits each time.
Make
(a) the second largest number
(b) the second smallest number.

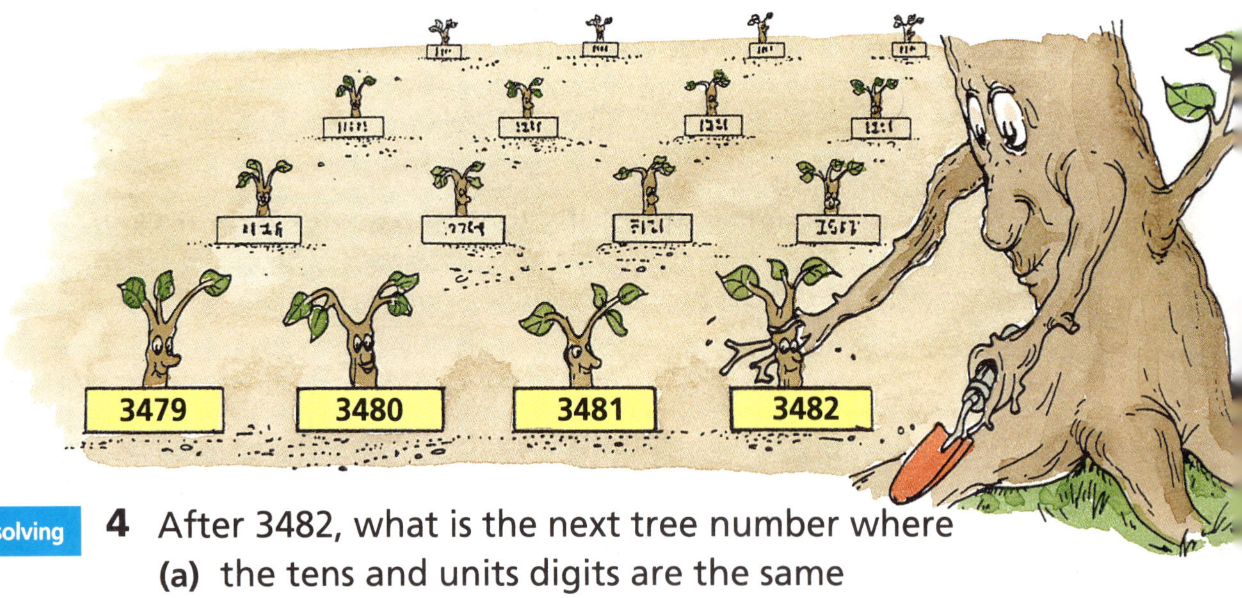

Problem solving

4 After 3482, what is the next tree number where
(a) the tens and units digits are the same
(b) the hundreds and tens digits are the same
(c) the hundreds, tens and units digits are the same
(d) all four digits are the same?

1 Enter these numbers in your calculator. Record the displays.

(a) one thousand four hundred and sixty-two

(b) four thousand three hundred and one

(c) two thousand and sixty-seven **(d)** six thousand and one

2 Each tree starts with 6315. and adds. Find their answers.

3 Which tree would you use to work out each of these answers?

(a) 1203. → 1303. **(b)** 2104. → 3104. **(c)** 6021. → 6031.

4 Add one number each time. Write the number you added.

(a) 2161. → 2661. **(b)** 1030. → 5030. **(c)** 6663. → 6666.

5 Subtract each time. Write the number you subtracted.

(a) 7718. → 7710. **(b)** 2501. → 2301. **(c)** 2162. → 162.

6

Fir reaches the target 8000 in four moves.

1238. → 1240. → 1300. → 2000. → 8000.

(a) What did Fir add on each time?

(b) Find another way of reaching 8000.
Write what you added on each time.

(c) Start with 1742. and make 8000.
Record your steps.

R2

9 Under the Silver Toadstool

Addition of Th HTU

How many Millitrogs live in castles Moon and Star?

Moon	4 5 5
Star	+ 8 4 3
	1 2 9 8 Millitrogs

1 Find the totals for:

(a) Moon 4 5 5, Sun + 7 4 1

(b) Sun 7 4 1, Star + 8 4 3

(c) Cloud 9 2 8, Moon + 4 5 5

(d) Rain 5 9 6, Star + 8 4 3

(e) Moon 4 5 5, Rain + 5 9 6

(f) Rain 5 9 6, Sun + 7 4 1

(g) Star 8 4 3, Cloud + 9 2 8

(h) Cloud 9 2 8, Rain + 5 9 6

(i) Sun 7 4 1, Cloud + 9 2 8

2 Find the totals for:

(a) Star, Cloud and Sun

(b) Moon, Rain and Star

(c) Rain, Cloud and Moon

(d) Sun, Star and Moon.

Problem solving

3 **(a)** Which three castles were destroyed?

(b) 850 homeless Millitrogs go to **each** of the remaining castles. Tents are set up for another 460. Are any Millitrogs still homeless?

Trog News

THREE CASTLES DESTROYED!
2180 Millitrogs made homeless

A fire, started by a sneeze from a passing dragon, last night destroyed

The banquet

1 Find the total number of worm whirlies on the plates of

(a) Kelvin	(b) Tony	(c) Lisa	(d) Kate
2421	4543	3621	4847
+3567	+3725	+1554	+3922

2 Find the total number of bottles of nectar fizz drunk by:

(a) Kelvin	(b) Tony	(c) Lisa	(d) Kate
4837	2286	5709	4685
+4354	+3938	+1597	+3325

$$\begin{array}{r} 354 \\ 9 \\ 7567 \\ +\quad 76 \\ \hline 8006 \\ \hline \end{array}$$

3 Find the number of each colour of milligums.

(a) Blue: 3568 + 542 + 6 + 87
(b) Pink: 425 + 5387 + 43 + 8
(c) Red: 4563 + 3 + 2150 + 88
(d) White: 7602 + 65 + 7 + 254
(e) Green: 6 + 304 + 8241 + 99
(f) Grey: 3945 + 657 + 3 + 5243

4 **(a)** What digits do ▲, ■ and ● represent?

Problem solving

$$\begin{array}{r} 4\blacktriangle5\bullet \\ +\,21\blacksquare7 \\ \hline 6519 \\ \hline \end{array}$$

(b) Use the clues to find the number of the key to the Great Store.

- The sum of the digits is 13.
- The number is less than 5000.

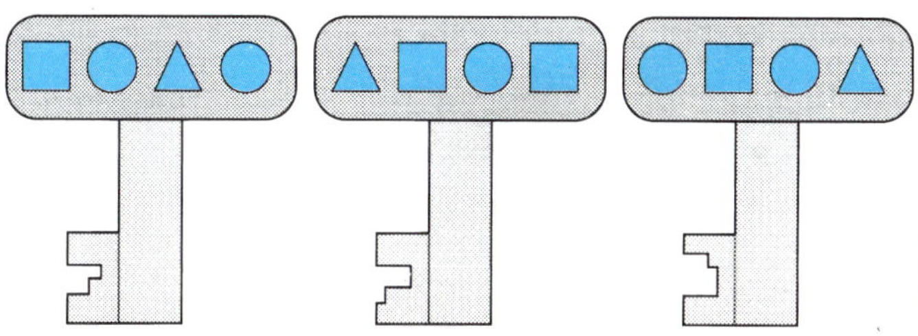

11 Subtraction of Th HTU

The Great Store

The Millitrogs keep a record of all the items used at the banquet. Find how many of each are left.

1

	Food	Before banquet	Used
(a)	acorn crunchies	4752	1520
(b)	pixie pasties	1379	434
(c)	hazlenut pops	5485	621
(d)	trog delights	3268	1533
(e)	milli whips	5057	3212

2

	Drinks	Before banquet	Used
(a)	cherry fizz	7471	5627
(b)	raisin riot	6032	2423
(c)	nutty nectar	4726	1850
(d)	berry brew	3578	1991
(e)	currant cola	7655	3684

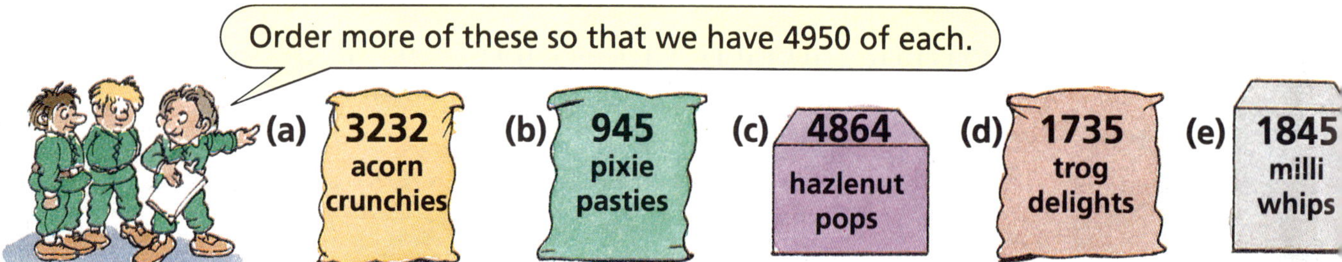

3 How many more of each have to be ordered?

4 The Millitrogs take these ingredients to the cook.

(a) How many more cherries than dates do they take?

(b) How many fewer raisins than nuts do they take?

Trog's Take-away

1 The cook and her helpers make a giant cake.
Find how many of each ingredient are left.

(a) raisins
$3892 - 1897$

(b) cherries
$6347 - 2569$

(c) nuts
$4426 - 1748$

(d) dates
$2675 - 1798$

They also make fruit drink and a large pizza.

Fruit Drink

2 Find the number of berries left.

(a) red
$2005 - 382$

(b) black
$3006 - 1573$

(c) green
$4008 - 1693$

(d) yellow
$6006 - 2216$

Pizza

3 Find the number of each ingredient left.

(a) onions
$3000 - 879$

(b) peppers
$4000 - 1437$

(c) olives
$2000 - 1562$

(d) mushrooms
$2000 - 155$

Problem solving

You can each have two sacks of milligums to take home. Their numbers must have a difference of 1789.

4 Which sacks could each take?

7157, 5367, 3682, 8946, 5471, 7224, 3578, 9013

Go to Workbook page 4.

Another adventure

The four explorers plan another adventure.

1 Find how much money each has.

Kate

Lisa

2 To raise more money they hold a sponsored disco.
List notes and coins they could use to pay for

(a)

Advertising
£11·25

(b)

Hire of hall
£12·52

(c)

Food
£15·84

(d)

Music
£16·70

3 The table shows the money collected.

Sponsors	Kate	Tony	Lisa	Kelvin
Neighbours	£8·94	£9·78	£9·10	£9·61
School friends	£6·22	£5·27	£4·94	£5·48
Family friends	£7·75	£6·66	£8·05	£9·20
Others	£9·16	£7·38	£8·02	£6·85

Kate collected £15·16 from neighbours and school friends.

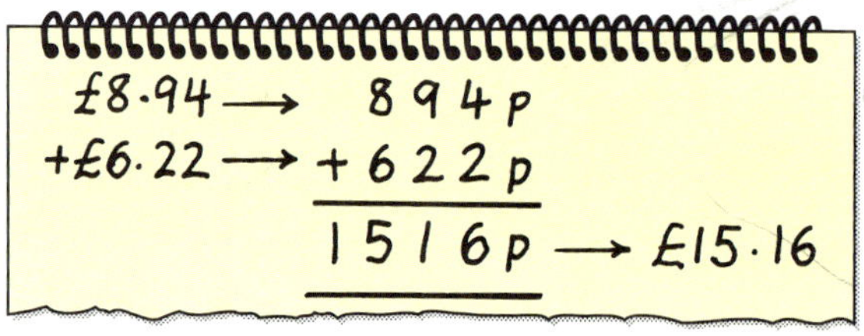

How much did each explorer collect from

(a) neighbours and school friends

(b) family friends and others?

1 Each explorer is given a £10 note to buy items for the first-aid box.

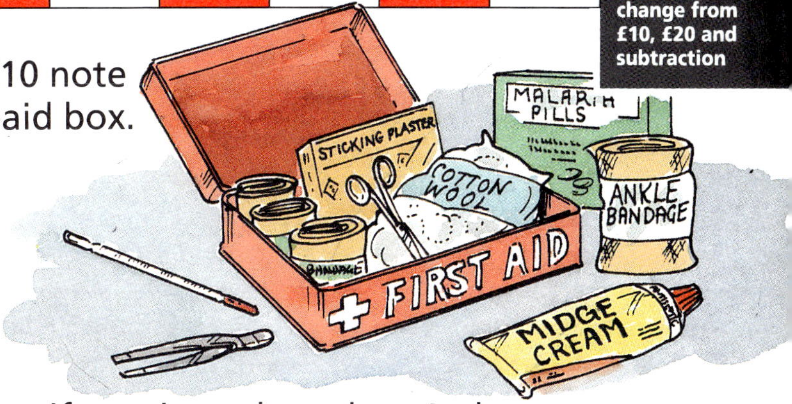

Lisa spends	£8·75
Tony spends	£7·68
Kate spends	£4·64
Kelvin spends	£2·43

(a) List the coins and notes, if any, in each explorer's change.

(b) Check each answer using a calculator.

2 Each explorer is given a £20 note to buy food.

(a) List the coins and notes, if any, in each explorer's change.

(b) Check each answer.

3 Find how much more each explorer spent on food than on first-aid items. Lisa started her answer like this:

Lisa
£17·88 → 1788p
− £8·75 → − 875p
→

Problem solving

4 Kate and Lisa each received £5 notes and 50p coins for their birthdays.

- Lisa has one more £5 note than Kate.
- Kate has twice as many 50p coins as Lisa.
- Altogether they have £31.

How much money did each receive?

Outward Bound

The children visit Outward Bound to buy equipment.

1 Find the total cost for each explorer.

2 How much change would you get from £20 if you bought the 5 cheapest items?

3 Sammi, Irfan and Suzi join the explorers.
Each has £20 to spend.
For each new explorer, make up an equipment list of 3 items and find the cost.

4 Rachel Rich, owner of Outward Bound, gives Suzi a voucher to buy one of each item in the display.
What is the total value of the voucher?

1 How much more does the rucksack cost than

(a) the ice axe **(b)** the goggles **(c)** the gloves?

2 Sammi has a £20 voucher.

How much would be left if she bought

(a) the trousers and gloves **(b)** the rope and torch

(c) the ice axe and map **(d)** the helmet and goggles?

3 Check each calculation.
Correct the ones that are wrong.

(a) OUTWARD Bound

helmet	5·72
gloves	4·38
rope	+10·60
	£20·70

(b) OUTWARD Bound

goggles	8·47
rucksack	11·51
compass	+ 2·63
	£20·61

(c) OUTWARD Bound

rucksack	11·51
torch	2·28
gloves	4·38
socks	+ 3·00
	£21·19

(d) OUTWARD Bound

boots	18·44
jumper	9·06
torch	2·28
rope	10·60
map	+ 3·36
	£43·74

(e) OUTWARD Bound

	20·00
rucksack	−11·51
change	£ 7·49

(f) OUTWARD Bound

	10·00
torch	− 2·28
change	£ 6·72

(g) OUTWARD Bound

	50·00
helmet	− 5·72
change	£44·28

(h) OUTWARD Bound

	20·00
jumper	− 9·06
change	£ 10·94

4 Four explorers buy food for their next adventure.

Problem solving

Sammi spends £29 Irfan spends £22
Kate spends £18 Tony spends £31

The four agree to share the cost equally.

Help them sort out who owes money to whom.

Ask your teacher what to do next.

17 Pairing

Other activity: addition, multiplication

Patti finds the total of a set of **consecutive numbers** like this.

I add pairs of numbers. I begin with the first and the last.

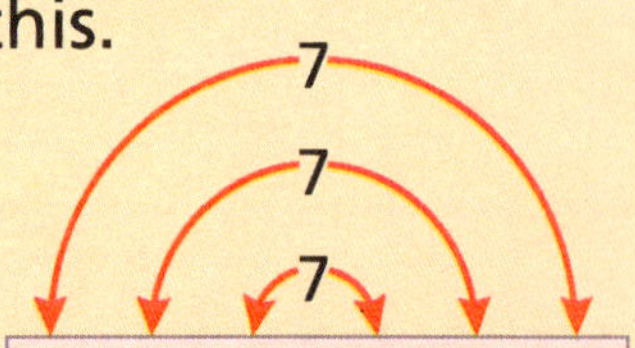

1 + 2 + 3 + 4 + 5 + 6

Total = 3 × 7 = **21**

1 Use Patti's method to find each total.

(a) 1 + 2 + 3 + 4 + 5 + 6 + 7 + 8

(b) 1 + 2 + 3 + 4 + 5 + 6 + 7 + 8 + 9 + 10

2 **(a)** Copy and complete this table.

Consecutive numbers	How many numbers?	How many pairs?	Sum of each pair	Total
1 to 6	6	3	7	21
1 to 8				
1 to 10				

(b) Write a rule to find such totals.

3 Use your rule to find each total.

(a) 1 + 2 + 3 + 4 + 5 + 6 + 7 + 8 + 9 + 10 + 11 + 12

(b) numbers 1 to 20

(c) numbers 1 to 100

(d) 11 + 12 + 13 + 14 + 15 + 16

(e) numbers 21 to 30

When I cannot pair **all** the numbers, I begin with the **first** and the **second last**.

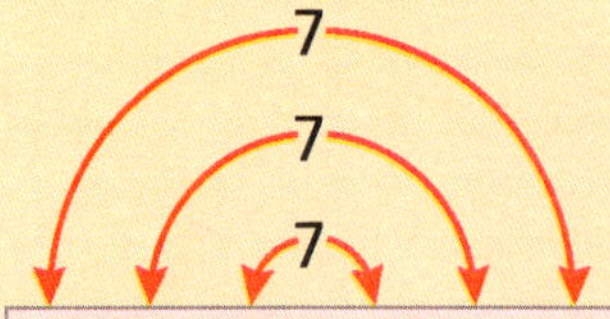

1 + 2 + 3 + 4 + 5 + 6 + 7

Total = 3 × 7 + 7
= 21 + 7 = **28**

4 Use Patti's method to find each total.

(a) 1 + 2 + 3 + 4 + 5 + 6 + 7 + 8 + 9

(b) numbers 1 to 13

(c) numbers 11 to 17

(d) numbers 31 to 39

Magazines

These children have made their own magazines.

1 Find mentally how many pages there are in these numbers of copies of

Emma's magazine	**(a)** 3	**(b)** 5	**(c)** 6	**(d)** 8
Ben's magazine	**(e)** 4	**(f)** 5	**(g)** 6	**(h)** 8
Shamina's magazine	**(i)** 4	**(j)** 6	**(k)** 7	**(l)** 9
Sara's magazine	**(m)** 2	**(n)** 3	**(o)** 7	**(p)** 10
Steve's magazine	**(q)** 2	**(r)** 7	**(s)** 9	**(t)** 10

2 Sara has 9 copies of her magazine.
Shamina has 8 copies of her magazine.

(a) Who has more pages? **(b)** How many more?

3 **(a)** A total of 36 pages is used for 4 copies of Sara's magazine.

36 pages ⟶ 4 copies of Sara's magazine

Find another **two** ways of having a total of 36 pages.

Problem solving

(b) Copy and complete.

49 pages ⟶ ___ copies of _______ magazine
38 pages ⟶ ___ copies of _______ magazine
and ___ copies of _______ magazine

Go to Workbook page 5.

Class copies

The table shows the number of children in these classes.

Teacher	Mr Kidd	Mrs Watt	Ms Smith	Mr Reed	Mrs Anwar
Number in class	27	31	24	30	29

Each child in Mr Kidd's class is given a 4-page magazine. Shamina calculates the total number of pages needed.

$$\begin{array}{r} 27 \\ \times\ 4 \\ \hline 108 \\ \hline \end{array}$$ pages

1 How many pages are needed to give each child in Mr Kidd's class a magazine with

(a) 3 pages **(b)** 5 pages **(c)** 8 pages **(d)** 7 pages

in Mrs Watt's class a magazine with

(e) 2 pages **(f)** 4 pages **(g)** 7 pages **(h)** 6 pages

in Ms Smith's class a magazine with

(i) 6 pages **(j)** 9 pages **(k)** 10 pages **(l)** 8 pages

in Mr Reed's class a magazine with

(m) 3 pages **(n)** 6 pages **(o)** 8 pages **(p)** 9 pages

in Mrs Anwar's class a magazine with

(q) 7 pages **(r)** 9 pages **(s)** 4 pages **(t)** 10 pages?

2 How many pages are needed to give each child in **your** class a magazine with 6 pages?

Problem solving

3 A **total** of 120 pages is used to give each child in Mr Reed's class a magazine.
How many pages are in the magazine?

4 **(a)** Which other class **could** also use 120 pages to give each child a magazine?

(b) How many pages would the magazine have?

Record Breakers

These children are preparing the school magazine.

PLAYGROUND RECORDS

Our playground is 110 metres long.
Here are the records set by pupils in our school.

Pupil	What they did	Number of lengths
Jenny	cycled	9
Shamina	balanced a book	4
Sharon	jogged	7
Sara	skateboarded	5
Ben	ran backwards	6

Jenny calculated the total number of metres she cycled.

$$\begin{array}{r} 110 \\ \times\ 9 \\ \hline 990 \\ \hline \end{array} \text{ metres}$$

1 Calculate the total number of metres for each playground record.

2 Calculate the total number of metres for each football pitch record.

FOOTBALL PITCH RECORDS

The distance around our pitch is 217 metres.

Pupil	What they did	Number of laps
Sue	carried an egg	2
Emma	bounced a ball	3
Steve	roller skated	4
Ben	go-karted	5

3 Calculate the total number of metres for each park record.

PARK RECORDS

Pupil	What they did	Number of lengths	1 length
Kay	leapfrogged	2	148 m
David	wheelchaired	7	106 m
Jonathan	rolled a hoop	8	103 m
Paulo	balanced a tray	6	115 m
Maria	walked on stilts	4	124 m
Yasmeen	dribbled a football	7	113 m

SCHOOL SCENE Collectors

Emma is planning a 'Collectors' page.

1 Write how many items are in each collection.

2 How many stamps are in each of these collections?

(a) Shamina .... 6 albums .... 125 stamps in each
(b) Lewis .... 5 boxes .... 178 stamps in each
(c) Steve .... 7 packets .... 142 stamps in each
(d) Sara .... 8 books .... 124 stamps in each

3 How many coins has each collected?

(a) Kay ... 3 jars ... 420 coins in each
(b) Sharon ... 5 trays ... 200 coins in each

4 Who should win the prize?

(a) Jenny ... 4 albums ... 327 photos in each
(b) John ... 6 albums ... 230 photos in each
(c) William ... 7 albums ... 189 photos in each
(d) Caroline ... 9 albums ... 146 photos in each

Problem solving

5 Find how many tapes Mohammed has.

SCHOOL SCENE

Spotlight On Sharon

BIRTHDAYS

- born 9 years ago today
- her dog, Spot, is 7 and has the same birthday
- Spot was bought on his first birthday

Use 365 days for each year.

1 (a) How many days has Sharon lived?
(b) How many days has Spot lived?
(c) For how many days has Spot lived with Sharon?

2 How many of each exercise does Sharon do in a year?

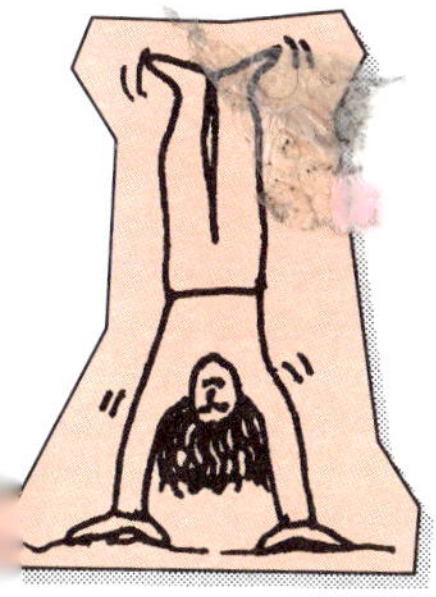

KEEP-FIT

Each day Sharon does
(a) 3 step-ups
(b) 5 stretches
(c) 8 sit-ups
(d) 4 handstands
(e) 10 press-ups

3 How many **minutes** does Sharon spend on each activity in a week?

SHARON'S WEEK

(a) Recorder practice	2 hours a day	5 days
(b) School	5 hours a day	5 days
(c) Exercise	1 hour a day	7 days
(d) Sleeping	10 hours a day	7 days
(e) Watching TV	2 hours a day	7 days

4 Sharon spends 5 hours with Spot each week.
How many hours is this in (a) 1 year (b) 6 years?

5 Gran is 8 times as old as Sharon.
Gran is 4 times as old as Hazel, Sharon's older sister.
How old is Hazel?

Problem solving

R7,8

23 Bundles

Multiplication: rule for × 10 and for × 100

1 Each copy of the school magazine uses 10 sheets of paper.

How many sheets are needed for

(a) 15 copies **(b)** 21 copies **(c)** 37 copies?

What do you notice about your answers?

When Ben multiplies 25 by 10 he notices

the units become tens

the tens become hundreds

there is an 0 in the units place.

H	T	U
	2	5
×	1	0
2	5	0

He uses a calculator for 37 × 10 to check if this happens again.

3 7 × 1 0 = 370.

2 Use Ben's rule to find the number of sheets for

(a) 26 copies **(b)** 39 copies **(c)** 30 copies **(d)** 28 copies.

3 Each bundle contains 10 magazines, each with 10 sheets. How many sheets are in each bundle?

Shamina calculated the number of sheets of paper in 13 bundles like this:

1 3 × 1 0 0 = 1300.

There are **1300** sheets.

4 How many sheets of paper are in

(a) 9 bundles **(b)** 23 bundles **(c)** 30 bundles **(d)** 35 bundles?

5 Write a rule for multiplying by 100. Check it with your teacher.

6 Use your rules to find

(a) 46 × 100	**(b)** 81 × 100	**(c)** 100 × 97	**(d)** 60 × 100
(e) 57 × 100	**(f)** 92 × 100	**(g)** 100 × 85	**(h)** 10 × 44
(i) 66 × 10	**(j)** 59 × 100	**(k)** 10 × 53	**(l)** 100 × 71

Speedprint

1 Class 5 visits Speedprint. They meet the manager, John Bull. How many copies of *Scream* are printed in 3 runs?

2 Find how many copies of each of these magazines are printed.

	Scream	*Puzzles*	*Champs*	*Monster*	*Soaps*
Number of copies in 1 run	1322	2124	2208	1246	1059
Number of runs	2	3	4	4	5

3 How many sheets are used to print these copies of *Upbeat*:
(a) 1138 **(b)** 1145 **(c)** 1156?

4 Find the number of sheets of paper used to print these magazines.

	Cool	*Galaxy*	*Charts*	*Donna*	*Stars*
Number of copies	1074	1106	1158	1167	1082
Number of sheets used in one copy	6	7	7	8	9

5 Which uses more sheets – 1194 copies of *Donna* or 1059 copies of *Stars?*

Go to Workbook page 6.

At the printer's

1 The cost of one print run of *Scream* magazine is £1124. What is the cost of 3 print runs?

2 Find the cost of printing each of these:

	Scream	*Puzzles*	*Champs*	*Monster*	*Soaps*
Cost of 1 print run	£1124	£1715	£1985	£1216	£1345
Number of runs	2	4	5	8	7

3 How much does Mr. Bull pay for 4635 sheets of paper?

4 How much does Mr. Bull pay for:

(a) 3275 sheets of plain white paper at 3p each
(b) 2480 sheets of glossy white paper at 4p each
(c) 1936 sheets of plain coloured paper at 5p each
(d) 1659 sheets of glossy coloured paper at 6p each
(e) 1105 sheets of extra thick paper at 9p each
(f) 1247 sheets of special paper at 8p each?

The cost of delivering *Scream* magazines to one shop in Largs is £13·45.

What is the cost of delivering to 5 shops?

£13·45 ⟶ 1345p
× 5
6725p ⟶ £67·25

The cost is **£67·25**

5 Find the cost of delivering *Scream* magazines to shops in these towns:

	Largs	*Girvan*	*Falkirk*	*Renton*	*Paisley*
Cost for 1 shop	£13·45	£15·69	£14·28	£12·39	£10·88
Number of shops	6	4	7	8	9

Making copies

Janice calculates the number of sheets the Mini can print in 30 minutes.

3 0 × 3 6 = 1080. It prints **1080 sheets.**

1 Find the number of sheets printed in 15 minutes by
(a) the Mini **(b)** the Midi **(c)** the Maxi **(d)** the Super.

2 How many sheets can each machine print in
(a) 25 minutes **(b)** 43 minutes **(c)** 1 hour?

3 How long does it take the Midi to print 6800 copies?

4 Each machine has a counter which shows the number of copies printed. Janice used the Maxi.

(a) How many copies did she print?
(b) Could she do this in 40 minutes?

5 Which machine can print 7128 copies in 72 minutes?

6 This is the counter on the Mini. Janice then uses the Mini for 18 minutes. What would the counter show at the finish?

7 Find how many sheets your school copier can print in 1 hour. Problem solving

27 Magazine costs

Multiplication: calculator, money

Teacher	Mr Kidd	Mrs Watt	Ms Smith	Mr Reed	Mrs Anwar
Number in class	27	31	24	30	29

The cost of printing a full-colour magazine for each child in Mr. Kidd's class is calculated like this:

2 7 × 1 · 3 7 = 36.99

The cost is **£36·99**

SPEEDPRINT

For printing *School Scene*

Charge per copy

Black and white	£1·05
Two colour	£1·13
Full colour	£1·37

1 For each class find the cost of printing when the magazine is
(a) black and white **(b)** two colour **(c)** full colour.

2 For full-colour magazines, what does Speedprint charge for printing
(a) 69 copies **(b)** 96 copies **(c)** 144 copies?

3 What is the cost of
(a) 11 full-page adverts
(b) 22 half-page adverts
(c) 7 full-page and 8 half-page adverts?

4 **(a)** What does the school pay for printing 500 copies of *School Scene* as a two-colour magazine?
(b) How much money does the school take in if there are 5 full-page and 12 half-page adverts in *School Scene*?
(c) How much does the school make by selling 500 copies of *School Scene* at 85p each?
(d) Does the magazine make a profit? Explain.

Ask your teacher what to do next.

Orders

Sara has orders for 128 copies of *School Scene*. Alan orders 4 more.

128 add 4. 28 + 4 = 32, so 128 + 4 = **132**

Alan adds in a different way.

128 add 4. 128 + 2 = 130
130 + 2 = **132**

1 Add mentally. **(a)** 132 + 8 **(b)** 246 + 5 **(c)** 229 + 8
(d) 173 + 6 **(e)** 230 + 9 **(f)** 182 + 7 **(g)** 202 + 5
(h) 244 + 8 **(i)** 119 + 4 **(j)** 306 + 9 **(k)** 496 + 6

Sara now has orders for 183 copies. Emma cancels her order for 5.

183 subtract 5. 83 − 5 = 78, so 183 − 5 = **178**

183 subtract 5.
183 − 3 = 180
180 − 2 = **178**

2 Subtract mentally. **(a)** 147 − 6 **(b)** 236 − 5 **(c)** 361 − 5
(d) 484 − 9 **(e)** 171 − 4 **(f)** 289 − 8 **(g)** 415 − 7
(h) 166 − 6 **(i)** 323 − 7 **(j)** 400 − 6 **(k)** 512 − 9

Sara now has orders for 250. Peter orders 30 more.

250 add 30.
50 + 30 = 80
The total is **280.**

3 Find mentally. **(a)** 130 + 10 **(b)** 160 + 20 **(c)** 240 + 30
(d) 120 + 70 **(e)** 210 + 50 **(f)** 250 + 40 **(g)** 160 − 10
(h) 150 − 30 **(i)** 200 − 20 **(j)** 260 − 50 **(k)** 270 − 40

Magazine sales

1 *School Scene* comes out four times a year.
Class 5 made this graph to show sales.
To the nearest hundred, how many copies of each issue were sold?

2 Round each of the following **to the nearest hundred.**

(a) 425 (b) 780 (c) 637 (d) 555 (e) 381 (f) 146

3 Use these enlargements from Class 5's graph.
How many copies of each issue were sold **to the nearest ten?**

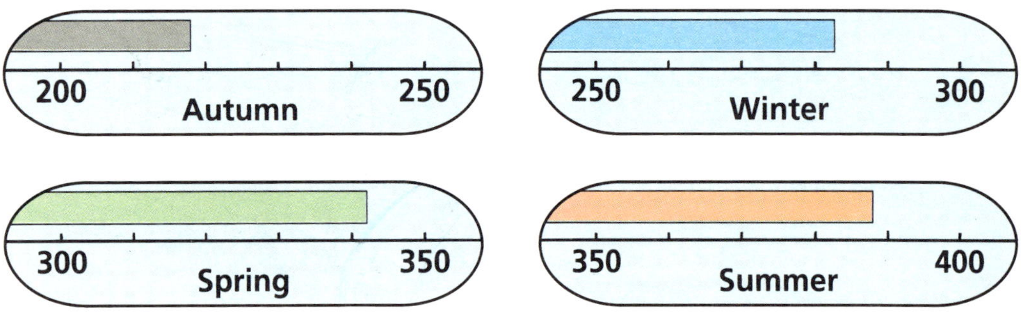

4 Round each of the following **to the nearest ten.**

(a) 423 (b) 637 (c) 781 (d) 552 (e) 388 (f) 146

5

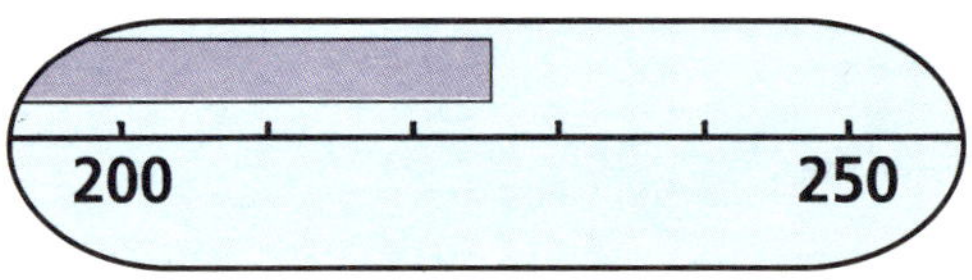

Who is correct, Ben or Kay? Discuss with your teacher.

6 Round each of the following **to the nearest ten.**

(a) 265 (b) 315 (c) 45 (d) 85 (e) 507 (f) 694
(g) 905 (h) 745 (i) 655 (j) 416 (k) 301 (l) 898

123 magazines were sold in January and another 69 in February.

Emma

123 is about 120. 69 is about 70. 120 + 70 = 190, so altogether **about** 190 magazines were sold.

1 Use Emma's method to find:

(a) 131 + 19	**(b)** 132 + 57	**(c)** 116 + 43	**(d)** 138 + 44
(e) 265 +21	**(f)** 111 + 43	**(g)** 326 + 35	**(h)** 17 + 221
(i) 24 + 108	**(j)** 75 + 404	**(k)** 222 + 66	**(l)** 36 + 158

178 magazines were sold in June **and** July.
62 of these were sold in June.

178 is about 180. 62 is about 60. 180 – 60 = 120, so **about** 120 magazines were sold in July.

Steve

2 Use Steve's method to find:

(a) 159 – 31	**(b)** 162 – 48	**(c)** 186 – 17	**(d)** 174 – 23
(e) 257 – 35	**(f)** 345 – 39	**(g)** 277 – 22	**(h)** 333 – 14
(i) 288 – 26	**(j)** 379 – 74	**(k)** 499 – 82	**(l)** 163 – 59

Month	September	October	November	December
Magazines sold	193	112	76	64

3 **(a)** **About** how many magazines altogether were sold in October and November?

(b) **About** how many more magazines were sold in September than in December?

Sales

Here are the sales figures for magazines sold during January and February.

	Scream	*Puzzles*	*Champs*	*Monster*	*Soaps*
January	2538	3151	3578	1584	2686
February	807	1433	992	2620	2869

	Cool	*Upbeat*	*Donna*	*Stars*	*Galaxy*
January	2847	3005	2353	2529	1294
February	1761	826	745	3471	2987

1 Which magazines sold more than 2750 copies in January?

2 Which magazines sold fewer than 1500 copies in February?

3 **(a)** Find the total sales of each magazine for the 2 months.

(b) Which magazine sold most copies?

(c) How many more copies did it sell than each of the others?

(d) Which magazine had the greatest increase in sales between January and February?

4 **(a)** How many more copies of each magazine must be sold in March to reach the sales target?

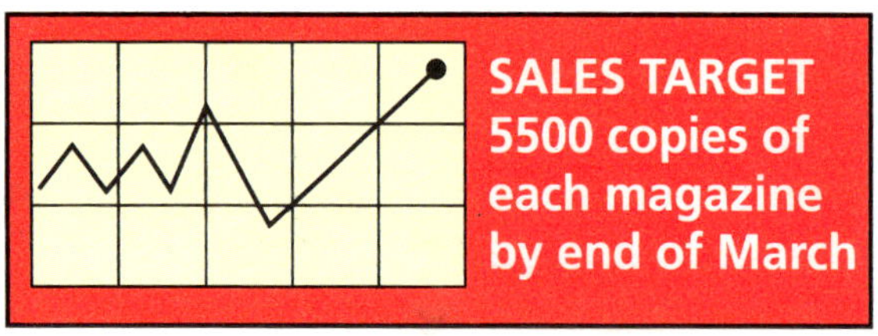

(b) One of the magazines
- sold more copies in March than in January
- sold exactly 5500 copies by the end of March.

Which magazine is this?

Ask your teacher what to do next.

Naomi's numbers

Naomi has a set of cards numbered 1 to 9.

She turns over these 3 cards. →

1 Using all three digits each time Naomi writes

- the largest number — 831
- the smallest number — − 138

Then she subtracts. — 693

↓

She uses the digits from her **answer** to do this all again . . .

$$\begin{array}{r} 963 \\ -\ 369 \\ \hline 594 \end{array}$$

↓

. . . and again.

$$\begin{array}{r} 954 \\ -\ 459 \\ \hline 495 \end{array}$$

What do you notice?

2 Do this with other 3-digit numbers.
What do you notice?

I wonder what happens with 4-digit numbers?

3 **(a)** Continue Naomi's working.
What do you notice?

$$\begin{array}{r} 9431 \\ -\ 1349 \\ \hline 8082 \end{array} \nearrow \begin{array}{r} 8820 \\ -\ 0288 \\ \hline 8532 \end{array} \nearrow$$

(b) Investigate these 4–digit numbers.

6 8 2 4   3 9 1 2   7 9 6 8   5 3 6 4

The number wheel

Play this game with a friend.
You need a cube numbered 5 to 10 and some counters.

Take turns to:
- roll the cube
- multiply your score by any number from the wheel
- cover this answer, if possible, on one of the squares below.

The winner is the first player to have four counters together in a line **in any direction**.

10	24	45	32	42	40	35	48
56	30	64	24	72	14	80	63
15	18	50	27	48	36	42	45
54	35	63	30	72	21	81	70
20	90	12	20	54	30	49	40
50	40	60	36	70	28	80	16
25	90	18	100	60	49	56	27

1 Divide equally:

(a) 14 planks between 2 floats
(b) 21 helpers into 3 teams
(c) 36 flags among 4 ropes
(d) 40 balloons into 5 lots.

$30 \div 4 = 7 \text{ r } 2$

$\begin{array}{r} 7 \text{ r } 2 \\ 4\overline{)30} \end{array}$

4 times what is 30?
4 times 7 is 28.
There are 2 left over.

2 How many are in each row and how many are left over?

(a) 19 stars in 2 equal rows
(b) 25 nails in 3 equal rows
(c) 42 chairs in 4 equal rows
(d) 49 lights in 5 equal rows

3

(a) $17 \div 4$
(b) $19 \div 3$
(c) $30 \div 5$
(d) $17 \div 2$
(e) $20 \div 2$
(f) $8 \div 5$
(g) $29 \div 3$
(h) $27 \div 4$
(i) $2\overline{)11}$
(j) $5\overline{)27}$
(k) $4\overline{)32}$
(l) $3\overline{)14}$
(m) $\frac{1}{5}$ of 25
(n) $\frac{1}{3}$ of 12
(o) $\frac{1}{2}$ of 18
(p) $\frac{1}{4}$ of 20

4 Find a whole number which divides **exactly** by 2, and by 3, and by 5.

Problem solving

35 Getting ready

Division: TU by 2, 3, 4, 5

Share 72 posters equally among 4 girls.

$$\begin{array}{r} 1\,8 \\ 4\overline{)7\,{}^{3}2} \end{array}$$

Each girl receives **18 posters**.

1 Share equally between 2 floats:

(a) 86 flowers **(b)** 54 balloons **(c)** 38 rosettes

2 Divide equally for the 3 days of the Carnival:

(a) 69 police **(b)** 42 traffic wardens **(c)** 78 stewards

3 Divide by 4:

(a) 68 tickets **(b)** 56 programmes **(c)** 70 badges

4 How many sets of 5?

(a) 70 hats **(b)** 65 masks **(c)** 91 arm bands

5 **(a)** $86 \div 4$ **(b)** $52 \div 3$ **(c)** $75 \div 2$ **(d)** $79 \div 5$

(e) $2\overline{)93}$ **(f)** $3\overline{)70}$ **(g)** $4\overline{)55}$ **(h)** $5\overline{)83}$

(i) $\frac{1}{2}$ of 58 **(j)** $\frac{1}{5}$ of 75 **(k)** $\frac{1}{3}$ of 81 **(l)** $\frac{1}{4}$ of 76

6 **(a)** On Thursday the video team records for 90 minutes. They divide the time equally among these 5 activities:

For how many minutes do they record each activity?

(b) On Friday
- 6 of the 90 minutes are spent having tea
- there are only 3 activities.

For how many minutes do they record each activity?

7 The team wants to record a total of 35 hours of tape. How many tapes do they need when they use only

(a) 2-hour tapes **(b)** 3-hour tapes **(c)** 4-hour tapes?

Go to Workbook page 8.

285 beads are shared equally among 5 costumes.

$$\begin{array}{r} 5\;7 \\ 5\overline{)\,2\;{}^{2}8\;{}^{3}5} \end{array}$$

There are **57 beads** for each costume.

1 Share equally among 5 costumes:
(a) 180 (b) 535 (c) 400 (d) 355 (e) 309 beads.

2 Stars are sewn in rows of 4.
How many rows can be made with
(a) 436 (b) 175 (c) 272 (d) 560 (e) 305 stars?

3 Each hat has 3 feathers. How many hats can be made with
(a) 114 (b) 207 (c) 173 (d) 471 (e) 160 feathers?

4 Programmes are shared into 2 equal piles.
How many are in each pile when there are
(a) 250 (b) 170 (c) 307 (d) 353 (e) 584 programmes?

5 (a) $\frac{1}{3}$ of 927 (b) $\frac{1}{4}$ of 824 (c) $787 \div 2$ (d) $983 \div 5$

(e) $4\overline{)709}$ (f) $2\overline{)943}$ (g) $5\overline{)649}$ (h) $3\overline{)512}$

6 Which of these numbers
(a) divide exactly by 3
(b) have a remainder of 1 when divided by 4?

7 Use the digits **1** **2** **5** **6** to make 3-digit numbers which

Problem solving

(a) divide exactly by 5

(b) have remainder 2 when divided by 5

(c) do not divide exactly by 2, 3, 4 or 5

Check that your numbers are correct.

Dragons galore!

1 Share coloured cloth equally among the 6 dragons.

(a) orange: 24 m (b) green: 36 m (c) blue: 42 m
(d) striped: 54 m (e) checked: 48 m (f) spotted: 60 m

2 Divide equally among 7 sections of a dragon:

(a) 21 hoops (b) 35 feathers (c) 42 balls of wool
(d) 14 tubes (e) 63 cards (f) 70 sheets of foil.

3 (a) $18 \div 6$ (b) $30 \div 7$ (c) $10 \div 6$ (d) $60 \div 7$
(e) $25 \div 6$ (f) $39 \div 6$ (g) $13 \div 7$ (h) $49 \div 7$
(i) $7\overline{)38}$ (j) $6\overline{)30}$ (k) $6\overline{)17}$ (l) $7\overline{)71}$

4 Chen Li collected these items to decorate the dragons.
How many of these can he make:

(a) bags of 7 nuts
(b) bundles of 6 straws
(c) strings of 7 bottle tops?

5 Gita uses 12 plates from a pack of 50. She then shares the rest equally among the 6 dragons. How many plates are there for each dragon? How many are left?

Problem solving

6 Divide 59 teeth among the 6 dragons so that one dragon has 5 more teeth than each of the others.

1 Share equally among the 6 dragons.

(a) 84 bows **(b)** 96 corks **(c)** 78 cotton reels
(d) 684 beads **(e)** 834 buttons **(f)** 565 bells

2 Share coloured ribbons equally among the 7 sections.

(a) 84 tartan **(b)** 98 striped **(c)** 81 red
(d) 756 spotted **(e)** 448 checked **(f)** 500 pink

3 **(a)** $90 \div 6$ **(b)** $867 \div 7$ **(c)** $925 \div 6$ **(d)** $99 \div 7$
(e) $884 \div 6$ **(f)** $795 \div 7$ **(g)** $999 \div 7$ **(h)** $630 \div 6$
(i) $6\overline{)200}$ **(j)** $7\overline{)322}$ **(k)** $6\overline{)705}$ **(l)** $7\overline{)915}$

4 Nick makes 3 types of patches to sew on the dragons.

7 petals

6 stars

7 circles

How many patches can he make with
(a) 495 petals **(b)** 608 stars **(c)** 750 circles?

5 Gita uses all these paper flowers to make 6 garlands. She shares each colour equally among them. How many peach, lilac and white flowers are in each garland?

6
- Gita has between 30 and 60 pink flowers.
- When shared equally among 6 garlands, there are 2 left over.
- When shared equally among 7 garlands, there is 1 left over.

How many pink flowers does she have?

Problem solving

Street decorations

1 Share these flowers equally among 8 barrows:

(a) 64 carnations **(b)** 40 tulips **(c)** 16 roses
(d) 24 daffodils **(e)** 80 daisies **(f)** 48 pansies.

2 Balloons are tied in groups of 9.
How many groups can be made from

(a) 36 **(b)** 63 **(c)** 45 **(d)** 81 **(e)** 90 **(f)** 54 balloons?

3 **(a)** $32 \div 8$ **(b)** $24 \div 9$ **(c)** $50 \div 8$ **(d)** $76 \div 9$
(e) $38 \div 9$ **(f)** $15 \div 8$ **(g)** $59 \div 8$ **(h)** $9 \div 9$
(i) $9\overline{)59}$ **(j)** $8\overline{)72}$ **(k)** $9\overline{)93}$ **(l)** $8\overline{)73}$

4 For the band, divide

(a) 35 bottles into rows of 9
(b) 68 bells into groups of 8
(c) 88 pipes into sets of 9.

Problem solving

5 Glee Street is 45 metres long. Lamp-posts are 9 metres apart.
A jester stands between each pair of lamp-posts.

Find the number of

(a) lamp-posts **(b)** jesters.

40 Division: TU and HTU by 8 and 9

1 Divide these items among 8 houses:

(a) 88 bows **(b)** 99 ribbons **(c)** 192 sheets of card
(d) 871 lights **(e)** 300 boxes **(f)** 970 bits of tinsel.

2 Divide these flags among 9 streets:

(a) 99 red **(b)** 153 yellow **(c)** 954 orange
(d) 703 green **(e)** 332 blue **(f)** 997 white.

3 **(a)** $90 \div 8$ **(b)** $100 \div 9$ **(c)** $879 \div 8$ **(d)** $562 \div 9$
(e) $777 \div 9$ **(f)** $374 \div 8$ **(g)** $949 \div 8$ **(h)** $108 \div 9$
(i) $8\overline{)968}$ **(j)** $9\overline{)895}$ **(k)** $8\overline{)807}$ **(l)** $9\overline{)989}$

4 Paula shares the coloured shapes equally to make 9 window decorations.

For each decoration, find the number of
(a) triangles **(b)** circles **(c)** rectangles.

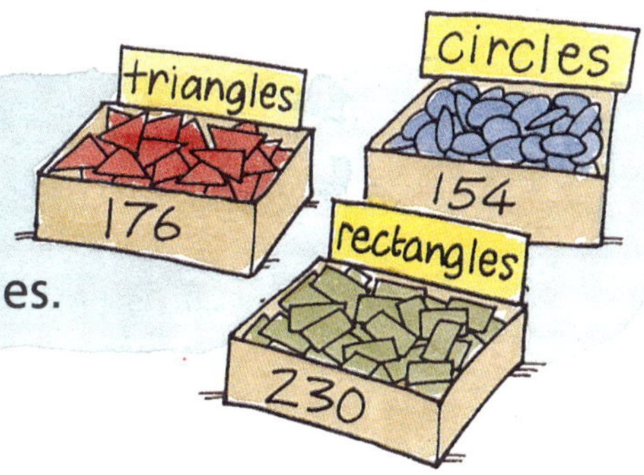

5 560 candles are put into 8 equal bundles.

(a) Paula takes one bundle.
How many **candles** does she have?

(b) She arranges her candles in sets of 8.
How many sets does she have?
How many candles has she left?

6 **(a)** Check that the jester is correct.

Problem solving

(b) Investigate this for these numbers:

279 **630** **747** **819**

(c) **Without dividing**, find which of these numbers divide exactly by 9.

275 **648** **536** **993** **702**

41 Litter

Division: TU and HTU by 10

The truck collects litter for recycling.

1 Divide into groups of 10:

(a) 60 cups **(b)** 80 cans **(c)** 100 leaflets
(d) 94 bottles **(e)** 75 packets **(f)** 66 cartons
(g) 90 tubs **(h)** 83 newspapers **(i)** 52 wrappers.

2 Cans are put in bags of 10.
Which of these piles will leave a remainder of 3?

3 Newspapers are put in bundles of 10.

How many bundles of 10 can be made from

(a) 170 comics **(b)** 280 leaflets **(c)** 315 magazines
(d) 494 newspapers **(e)** 675 posters **(f)** 800 programmes?

4 Look at these divisions.

$\begin{array}{r} 9 \text{ r } 6 \\ 10\overline{)96} \end{array}$ $\begin{array}{r} 12 \text{ r } 7 \\ 10\overline{)127} \end{array}$ $\begin{array}{r} 42 \text{ r } 4 \\ 10\overline{)424} \end{array}$ $\begin{array}{r} 76 \text{ r } 3 \\ 10\overline{)763} \end{array}$

Write a rule for a quick way to divide by 10.

5 Use your rule to find:

(a) $10\overline{)87}$ **(b)** $10\overline{)126}$ **(c)** $10\overline{)309}$ **(d)** $10\overline{)979}$

6 Ticket numbers that divide exactly by 10 win a vegeburger. Which of these tickets win?

(a) 364 **(b)** 450 **(c)** 505 **(d)** 712 **(e)** 900

7 Draw 5 tickets whose numbers have a remainder of 7 when divided by 10.

The procession

1 How many groups of 7 can be made and how many are left from

(a) 999 spectators **(b)** 793 marchers **(c)** 286 jugglers
(d) 502 musicians **(e)** 90 jesters **(f)** 265 acrobats?

2 Each juggler uses 6 clubs.
How many jugglers can perform if there are

(a) 737 **(b)** 679 **(c)** 93 **(d)** 453 **(e)** 188 clubs?

3 How many of the 502 musicians are left when they are put in groups of

(a) 8 **(b)** 2 **(c)** 3 **(d)** 9 **(e)** 4?

4 How many of the 793 marchers are left when they march in rows of

(a) 5 **(b)** 9 **(c)** 4 **(d)** 8 **(e)** 3?

5 One bottle holds 10 glassfuls. How many bottles would be needed to give a glassful each to

(a) 700 spectators **(b)** 89 jugglers **(c)** 151 acrobats?

Problem solving

6 There are fewer than 50 drummers.
When arranged
- in rows of 8, there are 3 left over
- in rows of 9, none are left.

How many drummers are there?

Go to Workbook page 9.

For each letter, fireworks are divided equally among the holes.

Letter	C	a	r	n	i	v	a	l
Number of fireworks	720	497	400	550	275	368	603	309

1 Find the number of fireworks in each hole.
Record your answers like this: **C ⟶ 120**.

2 Tickets for the firework display cost £3 each. Ticket sales raised a total of £975. How many tickets were sold?

3 Boxes of fireworks are used for the display.
Find the cost of each type of firework.

Firework	Number in box	Cost of box
Red Flash	8	£16·48
Blue Streak	6	£11·16
Silver Cloud	10	£22·60
Golden Shower	7	£15·89
Orange Burst	9	£13·50

Problem solving

4 **(a)** Which box of fireworks is the best value for money?

Explain your answer to a friend.

(b) What is the cheapest way to buy 18 Silver Fountain fireworks? Explain.

Ask your teacher what to do next.

Carnival jewellery

1 For each ear-ring, write
- the number of equal parts
- the fraction coloured red.

(a) (b) (c) (d) (e) (f)

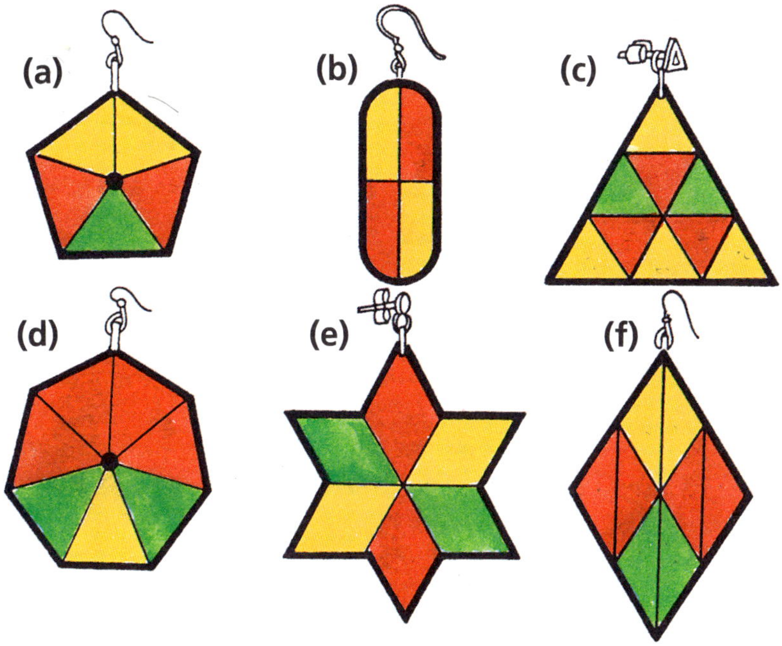

2 For each bracelet, write the fraction which is
- coloured blue
- **not** coloured blue.

(a) (b) (c) (d)

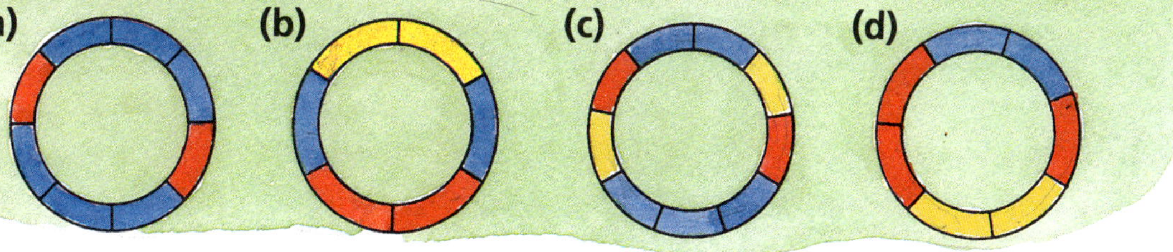

3 For each brooch, write the fraction **not** coloured green.

(a) (b) (c) (d)

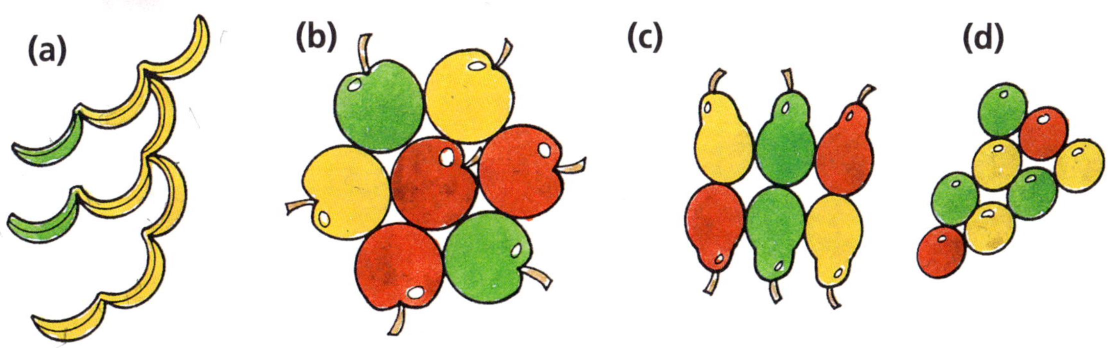

4 Design a piece of jewellery and colour $\frac{4}{9}$ of it blue.

More carnival jewels

1 **(a)** For each belt, write the fraction coloured yellow.

(b) Which is greater, $\frac{1}{6}$ or $\frac{1}{8}$?

2 **(a)** For each hairclip, write the fraction coloured blue.

(b) Which is smaller, $\frac{1}{7}$ or $\frac{1}{9}$?

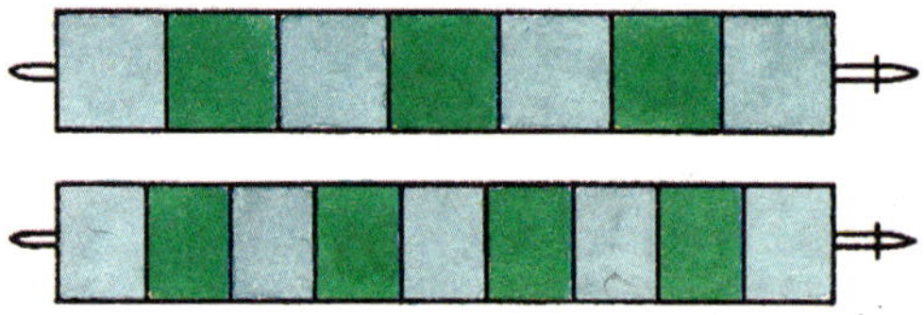

3 Draw the necklace with the fractions in order, starting with the smallest.

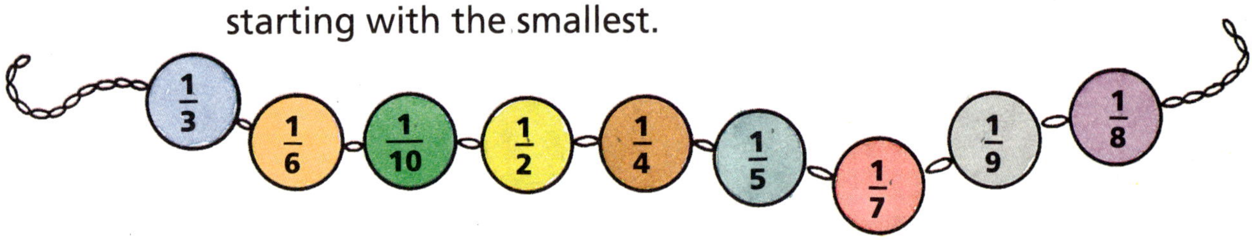

4 Fold a rectangular strip of paper into 6 equal parts. Draw a design for a hairclip showing sixths.

One sixth of the rings have red stones.

$\frac{1}{6}$ of 18 = 3

To find $\frac{1}{6}$, divide by 6.

5 Find:

(a) $\frac{1}{6}$ of 30 **(b)** $\frac{1}{6}$ of 42 **(c)** $\frac{1}{6}$ of 54

(d) $\frac{1}{8}$ of 40 **(e)** $\frac{1}{7}$ of 63 **(f)** $\frac{1}{9}$ of 45

(g) $\frac{1}{7}$ of 28 **(h)** $\frac{1}{9}$ of 81 **(i)** $\frac{1}{8}$ of 64

6 There are 48 necklaces in a box.
$\frac{1}{6}$ of them are gold, $\frac{1}{8}$ are silver and the rest are copper.

How many are **(a)** gold **(b)** silver **(c)** copper?

Go to Workbook page 11.

1 **(a)** Copy this grid on squared paper.

(b) • **Multiply** a pair of numbers.
• **Divide your answer by 6.**
• Write the **remainder** in the box.
For example, 4 × 2 = 8
and 8 ÷ 6 = 1 r [2]

(c) Complete the table.

(d) Write about any number patterns you see.

×	1	2	3	4	5
1					
2					
3					
4		2			
5					

Even numbers are red.
Odd numbers are blue.

2 What colour would the answer to an even number times an odd number be?

* means + or − or × or ÷

3 Find the missing signs.

(a) 26 * 13 = 39

(b) 9 * 9 = 81

(c) 27 * 3 = 9

(d) 92 * 10 = 920

(e) 870 * 10 = 860

(f) 870 * 10 = 87

(g) 8 * 2 = 16 * 4

□ stands for a number.

4 Find the missing numbers.

(a) $\begin{array}{r} 1\,1 \\ 7\overline{)\square\,7} \end{array}$

(b) $\begin{array}{r} 1\,4 \\ 7\overline{)9\,\square} \end{array}$

(c) $\begin{array}{r} 1\,2 \\ 7\overline{)\square\,4} \end{array}$

(d) $\begin{array}{r} 1\,3 \\ 7\overline{)\square\,1} \end{array}$

(e) $\begin{array}{r} 1\,3 \text{ r } 4 \\ 7\overline{)\square\,5} \end{array}$

Professor KLULESS

Professor Kluless is very absent-minded.

Help him solve these problems.

Collect a letter or word for each problem you solve.

1 On Monday he lost his answer sheet for this question.

Collect I

(a) Copy and complete:

3 × 37 =

6 × 37 =

9 × 37 =

12 × 37 =

(b) What do you notice about your answers?

(c) Write the next 5 lines and check your answers.

2 On Tuesday he typed ✻ instead of + or – or ×.

Collect a letter for the sign used most often.

+	–	×
C	B	T

✻ stands for + or – or ×

Find the missing signs.

(a) 53 ✻ 36 ✻ 29 = 118

(b) 53 ✻ 36 ✻ 29 = 60

(c) 53 ✻ 36 ✻ 29 = 1879

(d) 53 ✻ 36 ✻ 29 = 1937

3 On Wednesday, Professor Kluless could not remember how many crocuses he had planted in the laboratory garden. He knew there was 1 purple one for every 5 yellow ones.
How many did he plant altogether?

For 1205 collect A
For 1206 collect U

4 On Thursday he forgot his assistant Zantha's phone number.

Her number is ☐21 and divides exactly by 9.
Find ☐.

☐	1	2	3	4	5	6	7	8	9
Collect	**D**	**K**	**E**	**M**	**P**	**R**	**S**	**W**	**Z**

1st offer
£8 a week for 16 weeks

2nd offer
£1 for the first week
£2 for the second week
£3 for the third week
... and so on for 16 weeks

5 On Friday he offered Zantha 2 different pay rises. Which is the better offer?

1st offer collect **NOT**
2nd offer collect **VERY**

6 On Saturday the Professor ordered plain and spotted bow ties.

Altogether he ordered **12 ties** for £59.
How many ties of each type did he order?

Plain ties ordered
6 or less, collect **YYYs**
7 or more, collect **XXXs**

7 Use the letters and words you collected to find a message from the Professor.

The Professor's Safe

1 Start with the red panel. Use its answer to find the next panel to press. Record the sequence like this:

Colour		**Answer**
red	⟶	245
purple	⟶	

Divide **490** by **7**	Add half of **302** to **450**	**595** add **406**	**245** ÷ **5**
Find $\frac{1}{4}$ of **952**	$8\overline{)4760}$	**49 × 10**	Multiply **70** by **13**, then add **90**
1000 − 698	Multiply **35** by **7**	Double **601** and subtract **250**	**238 × 20**

2 There is a broken calculator in the safe. Only these keys work. **4** **5** **+** **−** **×** **=**

Use only these keys as many times as you like. Show the Professor how to

(a) make all the numbers from 0 to 20 **(b)** make 100.

3 Zantha finds a puzzle in the safe. Help her to solve it.

Use only 4 squares each time. Find paths from *Start* to *Finish*.

Find:

(a) the red path with the greatest total

(b) the yellow path with the smallest total

(c) any path where each number divides exactly by 7.

Finish			
124	161	113	88
84	99	49	105
103	133	77	206
141	217	126	231
Start			

The Kluless game

You need a calculator and counters.

Play the Kluless game with a partner.

- Take turns. Use the numbers and signs on the Control Box to make a number on the board.
- Cover the number you make with a counter.
- The first player to cover three numbers in a row wins.

Board

200	80	500
160	256	1
1000	1125	2000
625	10	5

CONTROL BOX

×	÷	=	25	16	4000
8	50	20	9000	250	

Ask your teacher what to do next.

HANNAH and BOB

A **palindrome** is a word which reads the same left to right and right to left. The names Hannah and Bob are palindromes. The numbers 919 and 3443 can be called palindromes.

1 Write some other numbers that are palindromes.

Hannah changes numbers into palindromes by **reversing digits and adding** like this:

$$25 \longrightarrow \begin{array}{r} 25 \\ +\ 52 \\ \hline 77 \\ \hline \end{array} \qquad 76 \longrightarrow \begin{array}{r} 76 \\ +\ 67 \\ \hline 143 \\ +\ 341 \\ \hline 484 \\ \hline \end{array}$$

25 is a **one-step** number because it takes 1 addition to make a palindrome.

76 is a **two-step** number.

2 Check that

(a) 13 is a one-step number **(b)** 56 is a one-step number
(c) 48 is a two-step number **(d)** 95 is a three-step number.

3 Change your own 2-digit numbers into palindromes.

Bob uses larger starting numbers to make palindromes.

$$367 \longrightarrow \begin{array}{r} 367 \\ +\ 763 \\ \hline 1130 \\ +\ 0311 \\ \hline 1441 \\ \hline \end{array}$$

367 is a **two-step** number.

4 Which of these is
- a one-step number
- a two-step number
- a three-step number?

128 1356 658 263

5 Find a 3-digit number which changes to a palindrome in
(a) one step **(b)** two steps **(c)** three steps.

Lewis Water

Four tenths ($\frac{4}{10}$) of this sail design are blue.
In decimal form, this can be written as **0·4**

1 How many tenths of the design are red? Write this as a decimal fraction.

2 These sail designs are divided into tenths.

Write the decimal fraction of each which is

(a) green **(b)** yellow.

At the club shop, milk cartons fill **1**$\frac{7}{10}$ crates.
In decimal form, this can be written as **1·7**

1 whole and 7 tenths

3 In decimal form, write how much of each item there is.

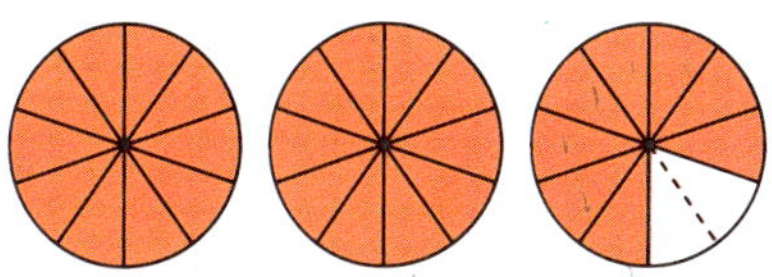

(a) pizzas

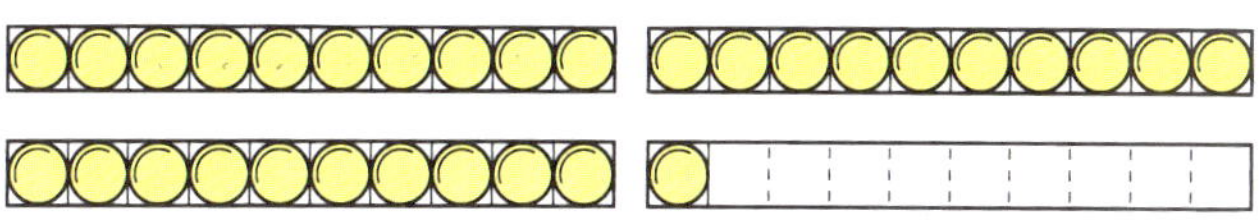

(b) packs of yoghurt tubs

4 Write in decimal form:

(a) nine tenths **(b)** $\frac{5}{10}$ **(c)** three tenths **(d)** $3\frac{1}{10}$

(e) two and seven tenths **(f)** seven and two tenths **(g)** $4\frac{1}{2}$

Go to Workbook page 13.

53

Decimals: tens, units and tenths

Balloon trip over Lewis Water

The fuel gauge shows that there are **1·6 units** of fuel in the tank of the hot air balloon.

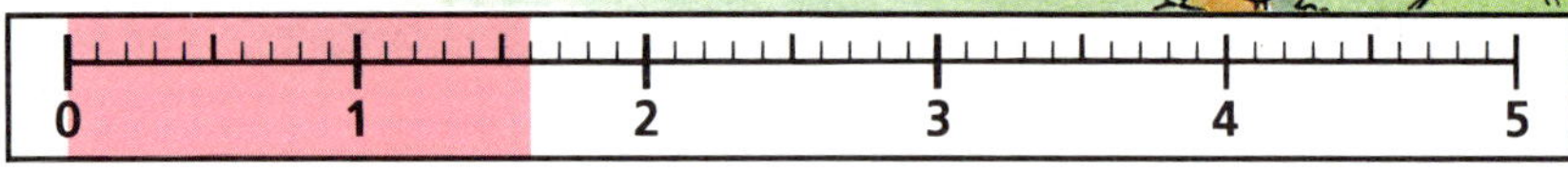

1·6 = 1 unit and 6 tenths = 10 tenths and 6 tenths = 16 tenths

1 Write these fuel readings in tenths.

(a) 1·4 **(b)** 1·9 **(c)** 2·8 **(d)** 3·5 **(e)** 5

This new gauge shows that there are **23 tenths** of fuel in the balloon's tank.

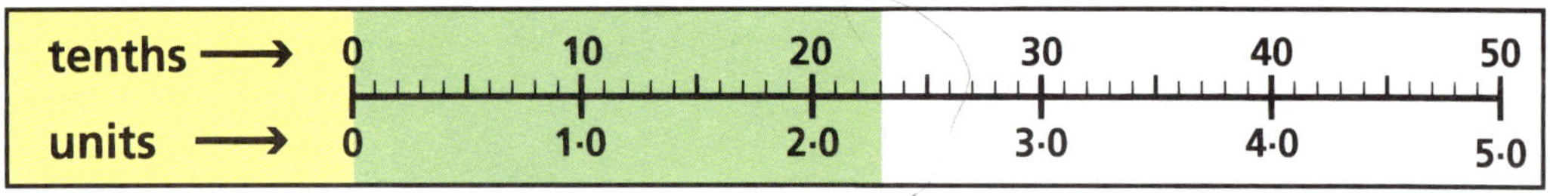

23 tenths = 2 units and 3 tenths = 2·3

2 Write these fuel readings in the same way.

(a) 29 tenths **(b)** 18 tenths **(c)** 47 tenths **(d)** 30 tenths

3 The table shows the fuel used on different days.

Day	Sun	Mon	Tue	Wed	Thu	Fri	Sat
Units of fuel	3·2	0·4	0·7	2·0	1·2	2·1	4·0

Write the units of fuel **in order** starting with the greatest amount.

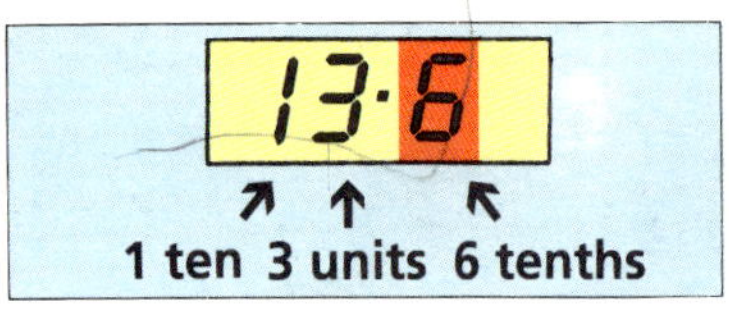

← The value of the red digit is 6 tenths.

4 What is the value of each red digit?

(a) 10·5 **(b)** 27·3 **(c)** 42·0 **(d)** 38·5

Go to Workbook page 14.

Boat repairs

Janet and Vijay repair boats.

Janet uses 2 pieces of cloth to repair the sail.
The pieces are 2·7m and 3·5m long.

Add the tenths.	7 and 5 is 12 tenths. Exchange for 1 unit and 2 tenths.
Add the units.	1 and 2 gives 3 and another 3 is 6 units.

$$\begin{array}{r} 3{\cdot}5\,\text{m} \\ +\ 2{\cdot}7\,\text{m} \\ \hline 6{\cdot}2\,\text{m} \\ \hline {\scriptstyle 1} \end{array}$$

She uses **6·2 metres** of cloth.

1 Add these lengths of sailcloth.

(a) 1·6m + 2·5m (b) 6·4m + 1·9m (c) 2·5m + 0·7m (d) 0·5m + 4·8m (e) 2·7m + 1·3m

2 (a) 4·5m + 2·6m (b) 5·8m + 2·4m (c) 2·3m + 4·6m + 1·7m
(d) 6·7m + 0·5m (e) 1·9m + 7m (f) 3·5m + 0·2m + 4·3m

3 Vijay cuts a rope into 2 pieces, 11·8m and 14·5m long.
What was the length of the rope before he cut it?

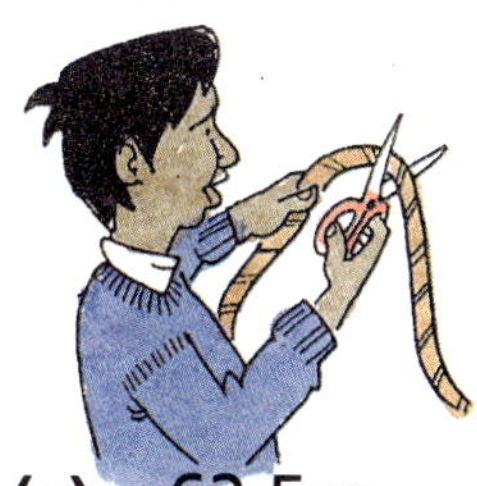

4 Add these lengths of rope.

(a) 23·7m + 15·4m (b) 14·5m + 32·5m (c) 41·3m + 25·6m (d) 35·8m + 7·2m (e) 62·5m + 8·8m

5 What was the length of each rope before Vijay cut it into these pieces:

Red rope	12·4m	1·6m	0·7m	23·5m	
Blue rope	18·4m	12·5m	3·9m	21·3m	10·4m?

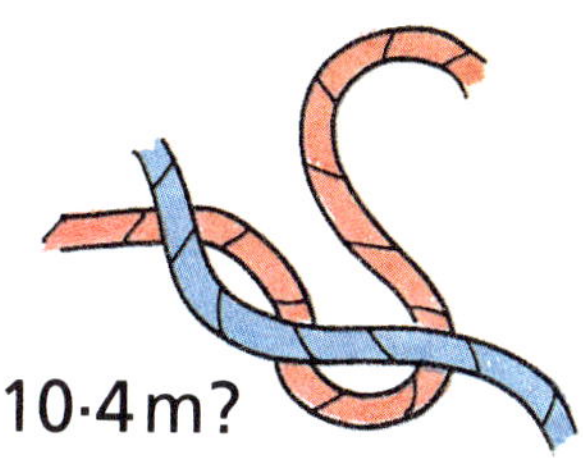

6 Which 3 pieces give a total length of (a) 12·9m (b) 15·8m?

Problem solving

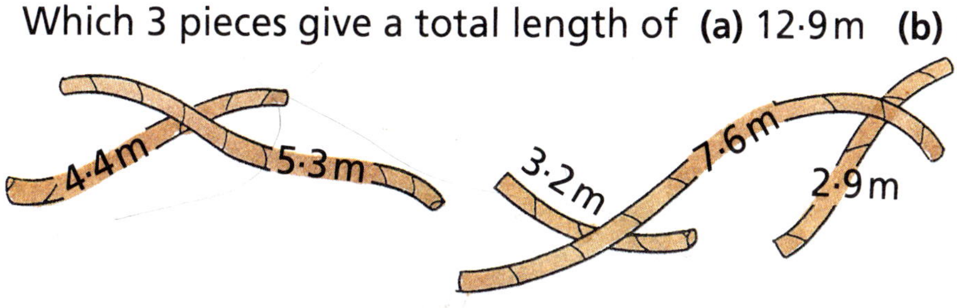

Model boat races

Fiona compares the lengths of *Sprite* and *Imp*.

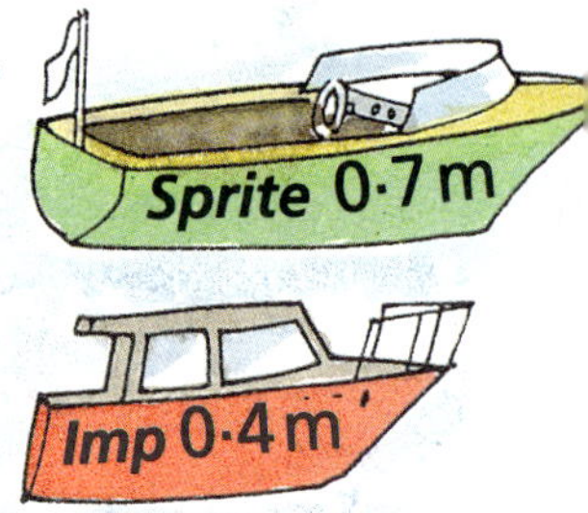

7 tenths take away 4 tenths leaves 3 tenths.
Sprite is **0·3 metres** longer than *Imp*.

1 How much longer is *Fairwind* than

(a) *Hope* (b) *Storm* (c) *Dawn* (d) *Imp?*

2 (a) Which is the shortest of the six boats?

(b) How much shorter is it than each of the others?

Rod's boat is 1·9 m long. *Sprite* is 0·7 m long.
Sprite is **1·2 metres** shorter than Rod's boat.

$$\begin{array}{r} 1{\cdot}9\,\text{m} \\ -\,0{\cdot}7\,\text{m} \\ \hline 1{\cdot}2\,\text{m} \\ \hline \end{array}$$

3 How much shorter is each boat than Rod's boat?

The race distance is **9·2 metres**.
When *Storm* wins, *Dawn* is 0·8 m from the finish.

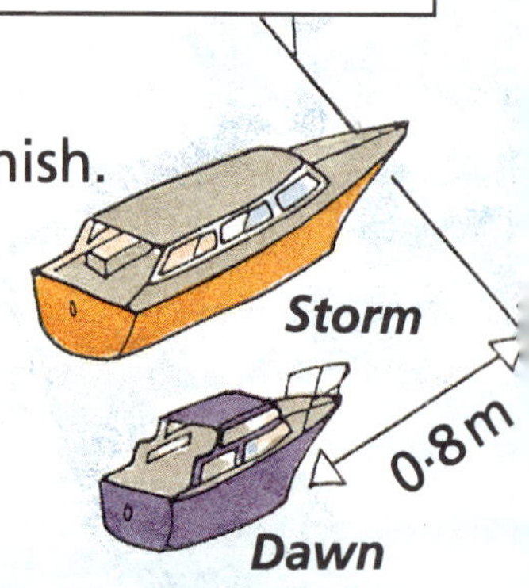

Subtract the tenths.
2 take away 8, I cannot.
Exchange 1 unit for 10 tenths.
12 take away 8 leaves 4 tenths.
Subtract the units.
8 take away 0 leaves 8 units.

$$\begin{array}{r} \overset{8}{\not{9}}{\cdot}\,{}^{1}2\,\text{m} \\ -\,0{\cdot}8\,\text{m} \\ \hline 8{\cdot}4\,\text{m} \\ \hline \end{array}$$

Dawn has sailed **8·4 m**.

4 Find the distance each boat has sailed when *Storm* wins.

Boat	*Sprite*	*Fairwind*	*Hope*	*Imp*
Distance from finish	0·4 m	0·2 m	0·9 m	0·7 m

5

(a) $\begin{array}{r} 8{\cdot}3 \\ -\,0{\cdot}7 \\ \hline \end{array}$ (b) $\begin{array}{r} 6{\cdot}5 \\ -\,0{\cdot}9 \\ \hline \end{array}$ (c) $\begin{array}{r} 7{\cdot}6 \\ -\,1{\cdot}8 \\ \hline \end{array}$ (d) $\begin{array}{r} 5{\cdot}4 \\ -\,4{\cdot}6 \\ \hline \end{array}$ (e) $\begin{array}{r} 6{\cdot}0 \\ -\,2{\cdot}9 \\ \hline \end{array}$

1 The second race is over a distance of **92·4 metres.** The table shows the distance each boat has sailed so far.

Sprite	80·8 m	*Dawn*	90·9 m
Imp	85·2 m	*Storm*	87·3 m
Hope	86·7 m	*Fairwind*	78·8 m

Find how far each boat is from the finish.

2 In the third race, each marker shows the total distance from the start. How far is it from each flag to the next?

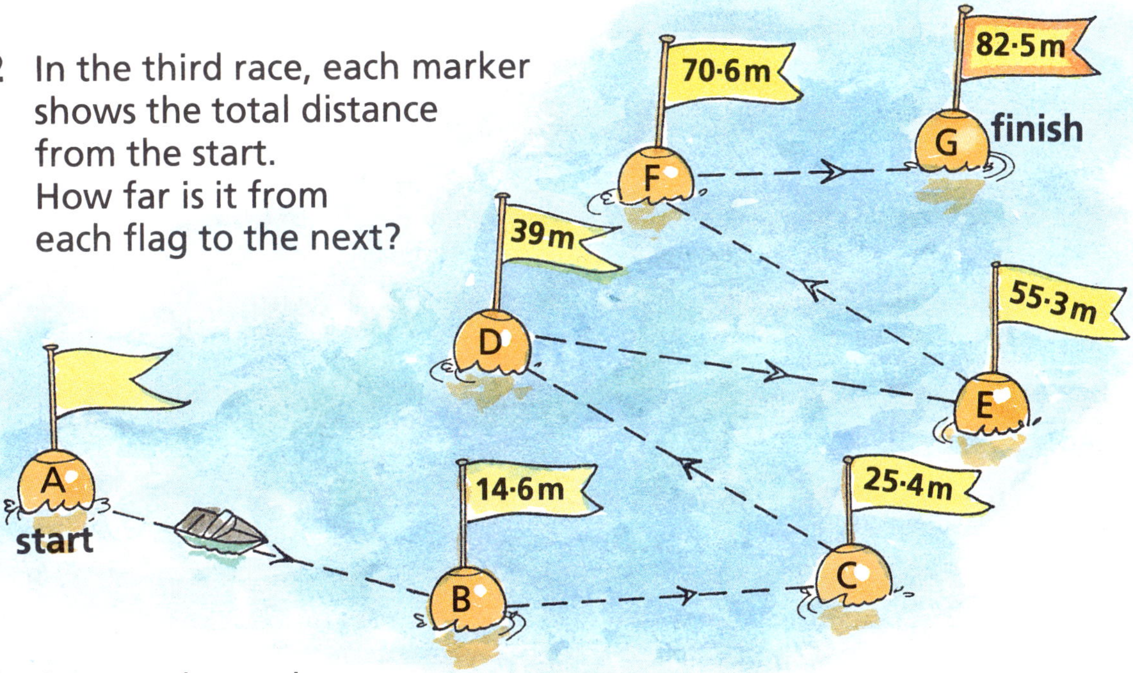

3 Copy and complete:

(a) $12{\cdot}6 - 0{\cdot}8$ **(b)** $14{\cdot}0 - 3{\cdot}7$ **(c)** $22{\cdot}4 - 10{\cdot}9$ **(d)** $23{\cdot}7 - 14{\cdot}8$ **(e)** $80{\cdot}3 - 25{\cdot}6$

4 Find the difference between:

(a) 14·2 and 0·6 **(b)** 0·4 and 18·7 **(c)** 26 and 3·7
(d) 14·3 and 57·2 **(e)** 90 and 0·6 **(f)** 72·6 and 8

5 Subtract mentally:

(a) 0·8 − 0·3 **(b)** 3 − 0·7 **(c)** 14 − 0·5 **(d)** 10·5 − 3·5

6 Three model boats have a total length of 2·1 metres. Problem solving
The blue boat is 0·2 m **shorter** than the red boat
and 0·2 m **longer** than the green boat.
What is the length of each boat?

Go to Workbook page 15.

Captain Hawkins' souvenir shop

Captain Hawkins makes shelves to display souvenirs.

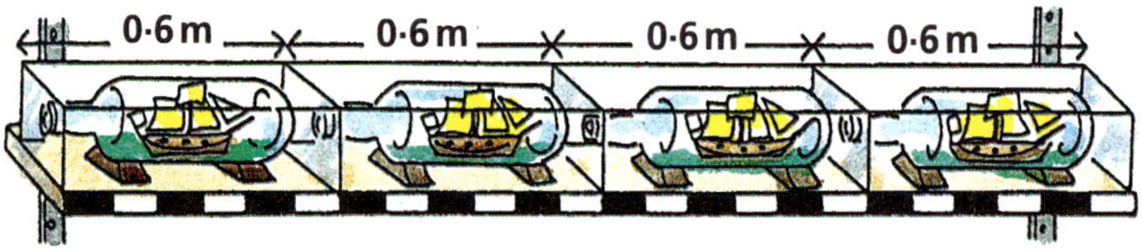

Each bottle is 0·6 metres long. He finds the shelf length needed for 4 bottles like this:

4 times 0·6
= 4 times 6 tenths = 24 tenths = 2·4

The shelf is **2·4 metres** long.

1 Multiply to find the length of each of these shelves.

(a)

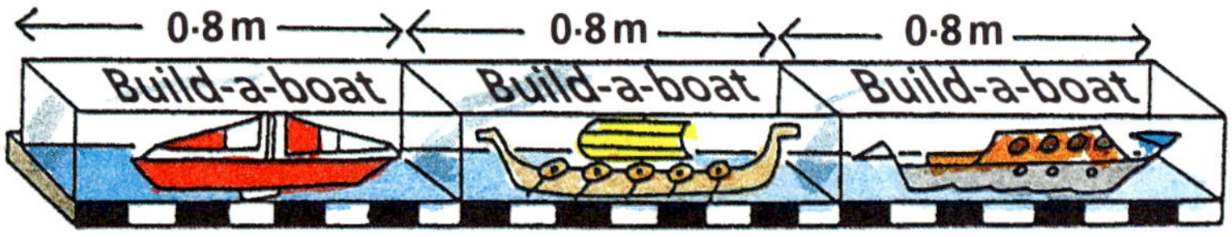

(b)

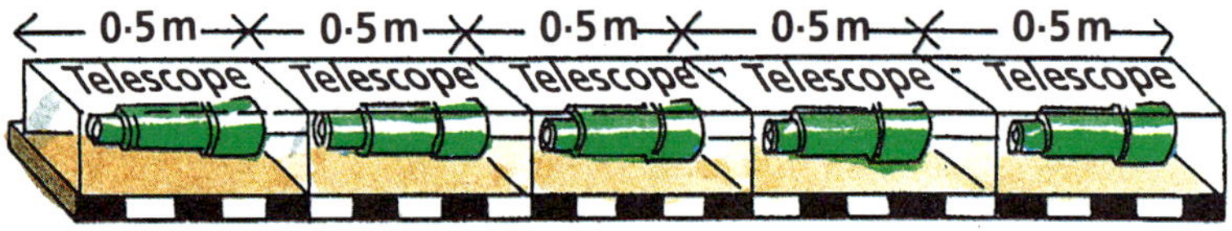

2 Find these lengths mentally.

(a) 2 × 0·9m **(b)** 6 × 0·7m **(c)** 7 × 0·8m **(d)** 9 × 0·9m

(e) 2 × 0·7m **(f)** 4 × 0·4m **(g)** 3 × 0·6m **(h)** 8 × 0·9m

(i) 9 × 0·6m **(j)** 5 × 0·8m

Each flag is 1·2m long.

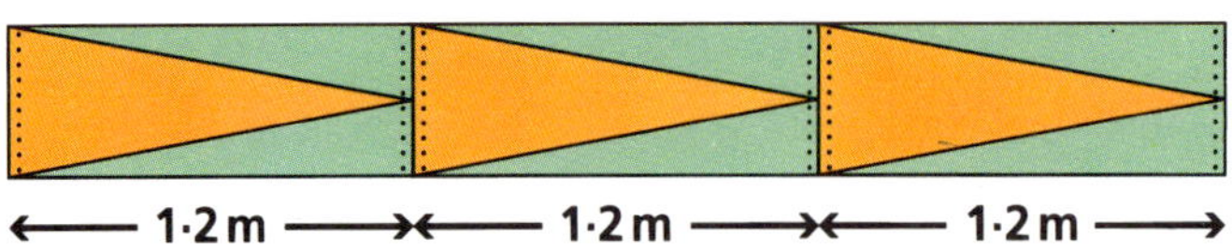

Captain Hawkins finds the total length of 3 flags like this:

```
  1·2m
 × 3
  3·6m
```

The total length is **3·6 metres**.

Multiply the tenths.
Multiply the units.

3 Find these total lengths.

(a) 3 × 2·3m **(b)** 4 × 1·2m **(c)** 2 × 3·4m **(d)** 3 × 3·2m

Paddle power

When Jason makes 1 paddle stroke his canoe travels 2·4 metres. He finds how far it travels when he makes 6 strokes like this: ⟶

$$\begin{array}{r} 2{\cdot}4\,\text{m} \\ \times\ 6 \\ \hline 14{\cdot}4\,\text{m} \\ \hline {\scriptstyle 2} \end{array}$$

His canoe travels **14·4 metres.**

1 Find how far each child's canoe travels.

	Jason	Eric	Monica	Carmen
Distance for 1 stroke	2·4m	3·4m	2·6m	1·9m
Number of strokes	8	9	6	7

2 Find these distances.

(a) 8 × 6·8m **(b)** 5 × 6·7m **(c)** 4 × 7·5m **(d)** 5 × 2·7m
(e) 7 × 6·7m **(f)** 5 × 4·9m **(g)** 3 × 7·5m **(h)** 2 × 7·8m
(i) 6 × 4·3m **(j)** 9 × 5·6m **(k)** 6 × 3·8m **(l)** 2 × 8·9m

3 **(a)** 4 × 13·2 **(b)** 6 × 14·1 **(c)** 10·7 × 8 **(d)** 3 × 27·6
(e) 13·5 × 7 **(f)** 5 × 19·4 **(g)** 7 × 14·2 **(h)** 16·4 × 6

4 **(a)** Copy and complete to show how far each child's canoe travels for 10 paddle strokes:

Jason 10 × 2·4m = 24m
Eric 10 × 2·6m =
Monica 10 × 3·4m =
Carmen 10 × 1·9m =

(b) What do you notice about your answers?

Carmen notices that when she multiplies by 10
- the tenths become units,
- the units become tens.

5 Use Carmen's rule to find **mentally**

(a) 10 × 5·7 **(b)** 10 × 8·9
(c) 10 × 0·6 **(d)** 0·8 × 10
(e) 10 × 15·5 **(f)** 30·7 × 10

R22

Spick and span

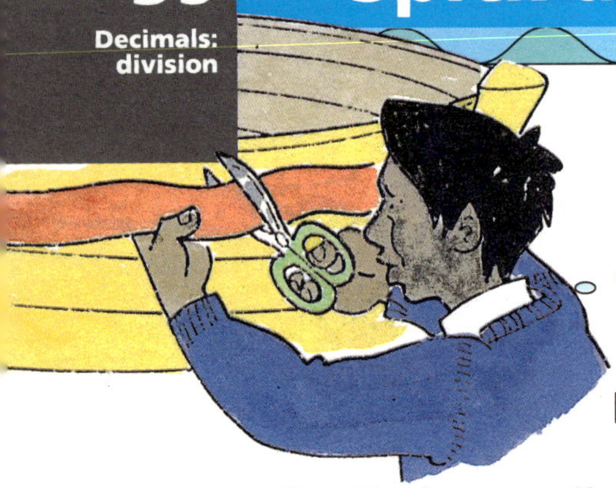

Vijay cuts a 0·6 metre length of plastic into 2 equal strips.

> 6 tenths divided by 2 gives 3 tenths.

Each strip is **0·3 metres** long.

1 Find mentally the length of each strip.

(a) 0·8 m cut into 2 equal strips

(b) 0·9 m cut into 3 equal strips

Janet uses 7·5 litres of paint to paint 5 identical boats. She finds the amount of paint for each boat like this:

7·5 divided by 5.

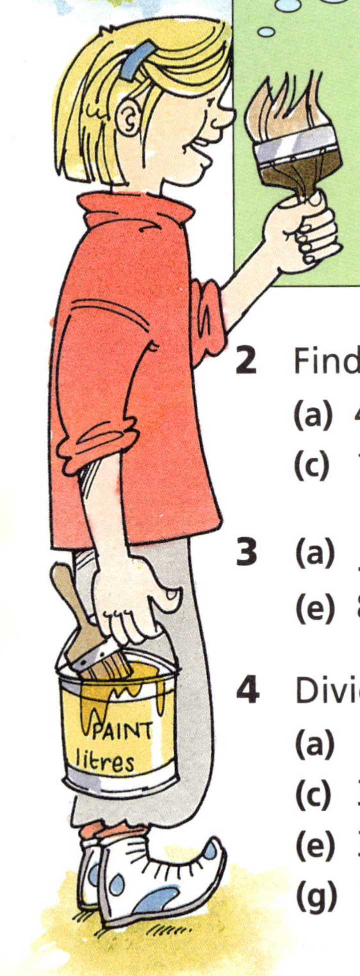

> **Share the units.** 5 times what is 7?
> 5 times 1 is 5 and 2 units left over.
> Exchange 2 units for 20 tenths.
> **Share the tenths.** 5 times what is 25?
> 5 times 5 is 25.

$$\begin{array}{r} 1\cdot \\ 5\overline{)7\cdot{}^{2}5} \end{array}$$

$$\begin{array}{r} 1\cdot 5 \\ 5\overline{)7\cdot{}^{2}5} \end{array}$$

The amount of paint for each boat is **1·5 litres**.

2 Find the amount of paint for each boat.

(a) 4·8 litres for 2 boats (b) 9·2 litres for 4 boats

(c) 11·2 litres for 7 boats (d) 15·3 litres for 9 boats

3 (a) $2\overline{)5{\cdot}6}$ (b) $3\overline{)7{\cdot}8}$ (c) $5\overline{)16{\cdot}5}$ (d) $4\overline{)3{\cdot}6}$

(e) 8·4 ÷ 7 (f) 9·6 ÷ 6 (g) 55·8 ÷ 9 (h) 37·6 ÷ 8

4 Divide these lengths of plastic equally.

(a) 8·7 m into 3 strips (b) 14·5 m into 5 strips

(c) 33·6 m into 8 strips (d) 22·2 m into 6 strips

(e) 39·9 m into 7 strips (f) 8·1 m into 9 strips

(g) 15·6 m into 4 strips (h) 14·4 m into 8 strips

Vijay shares 19 metres of bunting equally among 5 boats.

19 divided by 5.

19 can be written as 19·0
Share the units.
5 times what is 19?
5 times 3 is 15 and 4 left over.
Exchange 4 units for 40 tenths.
Share the tenths.
5 times what is 40?
5 times 8 is 40.

$$5\,\overline{)\,19\cdot{}^{4}0}\quad \text{quotient } 3$$

$$5\,\overline{)\,19\cdot{}^{4}0}\quad \text{quotient } 3\cdot 8$$

There are **3·8 metres** of bunting for each boat.

1 Share these lengths of bunting equally.

(a) 14 m among 4 boats **(b)** 18 m among 5 boats
(c) 17 m between 2 boats **(d)** 50 m among 4 boats
(e) 33 m between 2 boats **(f)** 69 m among 5 boats

2 **(a)** 42 ÷ 4 **(b)** 73 ÷ 5 **(c)** 84·9 ÷ 3 **(d)** 99·4 ÷ 7
(e) 50·4 ÷ 6 **(f)** 99 ÷ 2 **(g)** 90·4 ÷ 8 **(h)** 89·1 ÷ 9

Look for a pattern

3 **(a)** 23 ÷ 10 45 ÷ 10 71 ÷ 10 194 ÷ 10

What do you notice about your answers?

(b) Write a rule for dividing by 10.

(c) Use your rule to find mentally

34 ÷ 10 66 ÷ 10 80 ÷ 10 404 ÷ 10.

Try my puzzle

4 **(a)** Check that this is a magic square.

(b) Divide each number by 10 to make a new square.

(c) Is your new square magic? Explain.

24	3	18
9	15	21
12	27	6

Ask your teacher what to do next.

Taking stock

Multiplication: distributive law, × by 11 to 19

1 Help Captain Hawkins to find 13 × 15.

(a) Copy and complete this table:

Number of boxes	1	2	3	4	5	6	7	8	9	10
Number of caps	15	30	45							

(b) Use your table to find the total number of caps in 6 boxes + 7 boxes.

(c) Find 13 × 15 in two other ways.

2 Find the total number of stickers in 14 boxes.
Make a table to help you.

The Captain finds the number of stickers in 16 boxes like this:

$$\begin{array}{r} 18 \\ \times\ 6 \\ \hline 108 \end{array} \qquad \begin{array}{r} 18 \\ \times\ 10 \\ \hline 180 \end{array} \qquad \begin{array}{r} 108 \\ +\ 180 \\ \hline 288 \end{array}$$

There are **288** stickers.

3 Use the Captain's method.
Find the total number of items in

(a) 17 boxes of floats
(b) 12 boxes of hooks
(c) 16 boxes of flies
(d) 13 boxes of lines
(e) 15 boxes of floats
(f) 19 boxes of hooks
(g) 11 boxes of flies
(h) 18 boxes of lines.

Lewis Water Canoe Club

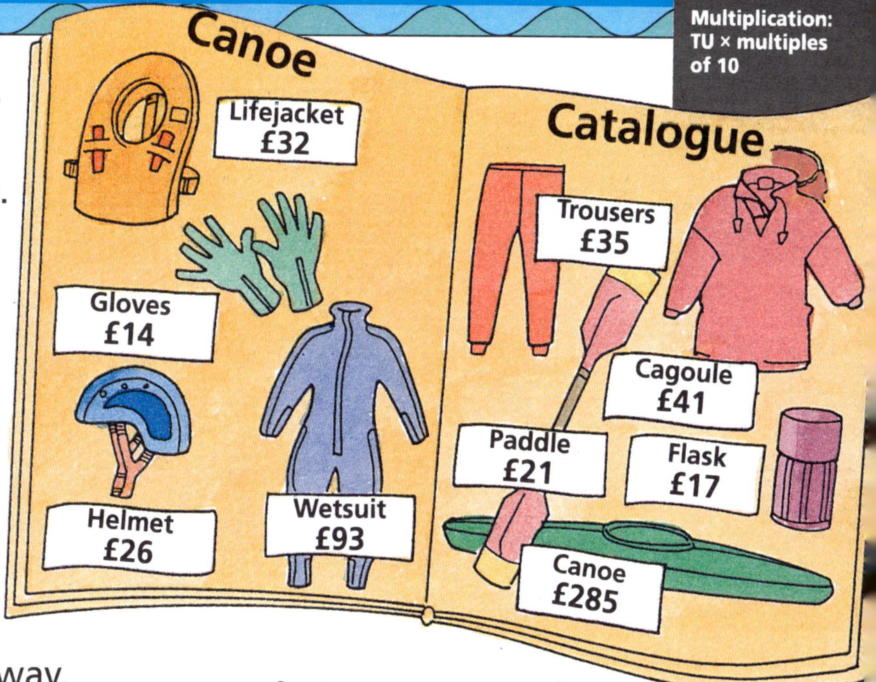

Jason and Carmen order 20 lifejackets for the Lewis Water Canoe Club.

Jason finds the cost like this:

$10 \times £32 = £320$

$10 \times £32 = £320$

so $20 \times £32 = £640$

Carmen does it another way.

20 is 2 lots of 10.

cost of 10		cost of 20
£32		£320
× 10		× 2
£320	→	£640

1 Use Carmen's method to find the cost of

(a) 20 pairs of gloves **(b)** 20 cagoules **(c)** 20 helmets

(d) 30 lifejackets **(e)** 30 flasks **(f)** 30 pairs of gloves

(g) 30 helmets **(h)** 40 paddles **(i)** 50 pairs of gloves.

Monica finds the cost of 20 lifejackets like this:

$$\begin{array}{r} £32 \\ \times\ 20 \\ \hline £640 \end{array}$$

Multiply by 10 then multiply by 2.

---

2 Use Monica's method to find the cost of

(a) 20 paddles **(b)** 20 pairs of trousers **(c)** 40 helmets

(d) 40 flasks **(e)** 50 pairs of gloves **(f)** 60 wetsuits

(g) 70 cagoules **(h)** 80 lifejackets **(i)** 90 helmets.

3 The cost of 29 of one item is £609.

Problem solving

(a) What is the item?

(b) Write about how you found your answer.

Regatta on Lewis Water

1 The length of each circuit of the canoe course is 32 metres.

(a) Copy and complete this table of course distances by **adding**.

Number of circuits	1	2	3	4	5	10	20	30
Course distance	32 m							

(b) Check your answers for • 4 circuits • 30 circuits by **multiplying**.

(c) Use your table to find the course distance for

• 21 circuits • 25 circuits • 32 circuits • 35 circuits.

The length of each circuit is changed to 35 metres.
Jason finds the course distance for 24 circuits like this:

4 circuits of 35 m + **20** circuits of 35 m → **24** circuits of 35 m

$$35\,\text{m} \times 4 = 140\,\text{m} \qquad 35\,\text{m} \times 20 = 700\,\text{m} \qquad 140\,\text{m} + 700\,\text{m} = 840\,\text{m}$$

2 Use Jason's method to find these course distances:

	(a)	(b)	(c)	(d)	(e)	(f)
Length of 1 circuit	35 m	28 m	46 m	25 m	37 m	43 m
Number of circuits	24	32	21	31	23	22

Problem solving

3 These six canoes are put into pairs for a relay race...

When multiplied, the canoe numbers for each pair give **720**.
Which canoes are in each pair?

Lady of Lewis

The *Lady of Lewis* carries
23 passengers on each trip.

In 14 trips she carries 14 × 23 passengers.

		23
		× 14
	4 × 23 →	92
	10 × 23 →	230
Add to find	14 × 23 →	322

She carries **322 passengers** in 14 trips.

1 Find the number of passengers she carries in

(a) 11 trips (b) 17 trips (c) 13 trips (d) 19 trips.

2

(a) 17 nights' bed and breakfast at £31 each night. How much altogether?

(b) 12 years old today. How many weeks have I lived?

(c) 16 days' holiday! How many hours?

(d) 18 crates with 22 cartons in each. How many cartons?

(e) 11 boxes, each with 36 bags of crisps. How many bags altogether?

(f) 19 days' pay at £34 a day. How much altogether?

(g) 15 adults at £25 each. How much altogether?

Ask your teacher what to do next.

Pirate treasure

Pirate's code

A	264	N	432
B	1930	O	672
C	570	P	324
D	405	Q	521
E	168	R	2106
F	4700	S	480
G	200	T	8600
H	72	U	375
I	42	V	1010
J	134	W	273
K	604	X	490
L	390	Y	80
M	192	Z	500

The pirates have hidden their treasure at one of the places shown on the map.
Find the answers to the calculations in this secret message, then use the code to discover where the treasure is hidden.

9 × 8	6 × 7	81 × 5	9 × 45	24 × 7	3 × 144		
10 × 57	18 × 4	4 × 42	96 × 5	86 × 100		3 × 14	48 × 10
4 × 108	112 × 6	9 × 234	1075 × 8	2 × 36		7 × 96	100 × 47
5 × 940	168 × 4	2 × 1053	5 × 1720				

Decimoles

Help the moles burrow underground by finding all the missing answers.

1

- 5·8
- add 4·7
- (a) ______
- multiply by 6
- (b) ______
- divide by 7
- (c) ______
- subtract 3·2
- (d) ______

2

- 4·6
- multiply by 8
- (a) ______
- (b) ______
- 28·9
- (c) ______
- 35·5
- (d) ______
- 7·1

3

- 9·6
- (a) ______
- 3·2
- (b) ______
- 8·1
- (c) ______
- 81
- (d) ______
- 40·5

POOLING IDEAS

Class 5 at St Andrew's School are asked for their suggestions for a new school pool. They visit the pool in nearby Greenburn to look for ideas.

1 List three different instruments the children could have used to measure Greenburn pool.

Work as a group.

2 **(a)** Measure, to the nearest metre, the length and breadth of your school hall.

(b) Check using different measuring instruments.

(c) Would the Greenburn pool fit into your school hall? Explain.

3 **(a)** **Estimate**, in metres, the length and breadth of
- a netball court
- the dining room.

(b) Measure these to the nearest metre.

(c) Check using different instruments.

(d) Would a netball court fit into the Greenburn pool? Explain.

4 **(a)** Try to mark out the corners of the Greenburn pool in your playground to see if it would fit there.

(b) Write about how you did this.

John is reading the programme for a swimming gala.

1 What length of pool would be suitable for all of these events? Explain.

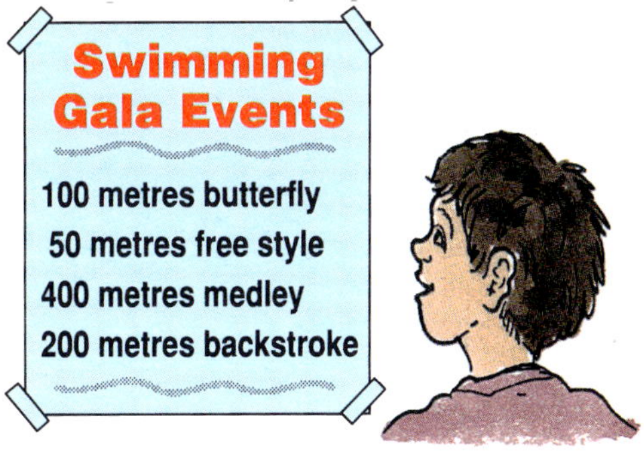

2 The new pool at St Andrew's School will be **20 metres** long and **12 metres** wide.

(a) How many lengths of this pool would be swum in a 200 metre event?

(b) Which event from the programme would be difficult to hold in the new pool? Explain.

3 **(a)** Greenburn pool is **33 metres** long. How many metres did each of these children swim?

Greenburn Pool Awards

Name	Award	Lengths
LARA	Salmon	1
ROB	Swordfish	2
KAREN	Shark	4

Work as a group.

(b) Mark out the new St Andrew's pool in your playground or school hall. The sizes are in question **2**.

(c) Use your marked-out pool. Show each child's **finishing position** if they swam the distances in part (a) in the **new pool**.

Problem solving

Work as a group.

4 Find the distance **around the outside** of your marked-out St Andrew's School pool. How many metres is it altogether?

The distance around a shape is called its **perimeter**.

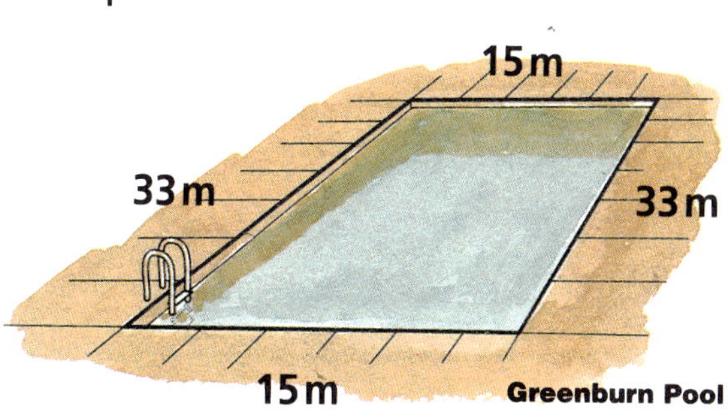

5 Calculate the perimeter of the Greenburn pool.

Go to Workbook page 16.

St Andrew's School pool

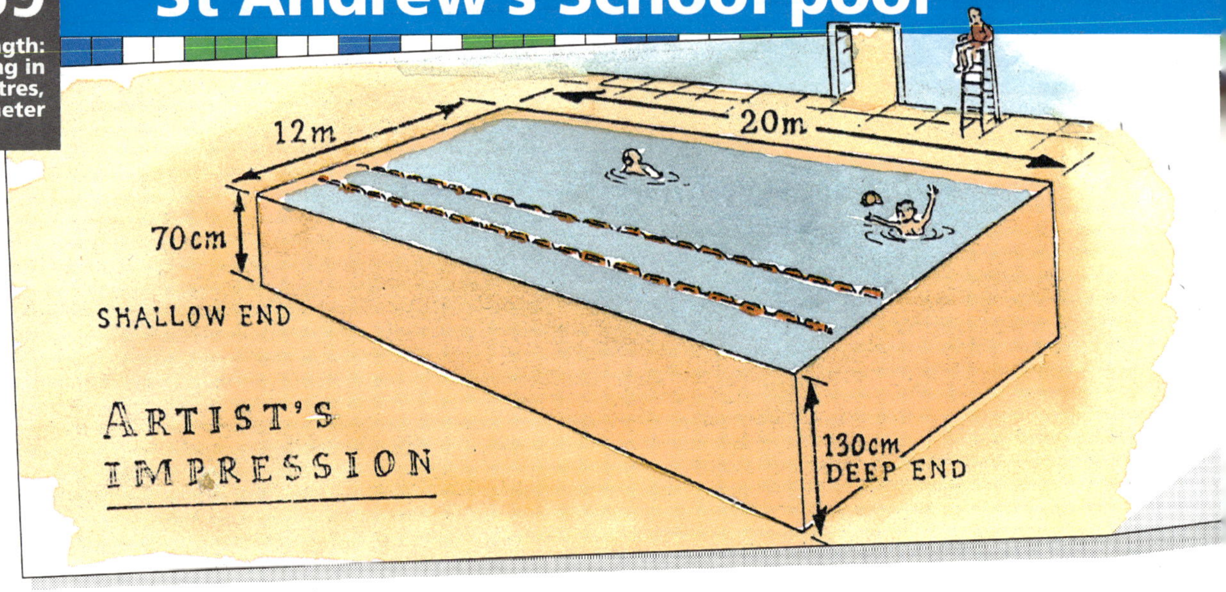

1 Work with a partner.

(a) What is the depth of the pool at
- the shallow end
- the deep end?

(b) Measure the height of your partner's
- knee
- waist
- shoulder
- nose.

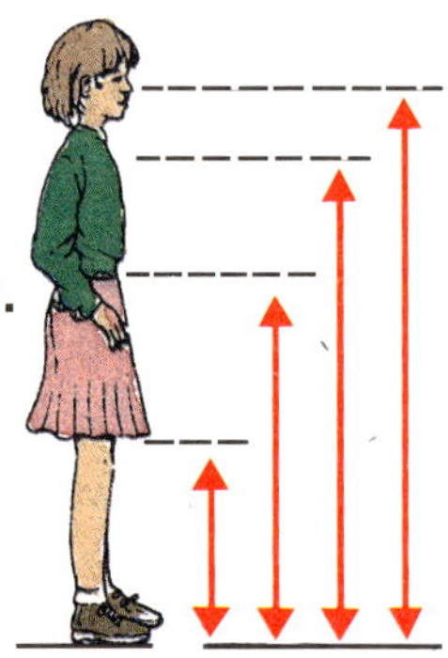

(c) Which of these parts of **your** body would be underwater if **you** stood in
- the shallow end
- the deep end

of St Andrew's pool?

2 What is the difference between the heights of **your**

(a) waist and knee (b) nose and shoulder
(c) shoulder and knee (d) nose and waist?

3 (a) Find the height of your teacher's
- knee
- waist
- shoulder
- nose.

(b) Which of these would be underwater if your teacher stood in
- the shallow end
- the deep end?

(c) Find the difference in height between each of your measurements and your teacher's.

Problem solving

4 Some swimming award badges are rectangles. On squared paper design as many **different shaped rectangular** badges as you can, each with a perimeter of 24 centimetres.

Glides and dives

1 Write each of these glide lengths in another way.

First glide	Naomi	Kris	Gordon	Marie	Rashmi
	435cm	497cm	3m 76cm	4m 29cm	3m 4cm

Jan's second glide was 3m 97cm.
She calculated the total
for her two glides like this.

$$\begin{array}{r} 309\text{cm} \\ +\ 397\text{cm} \\ \hline 706\text{cm} \end{array} \longrightarrow \textbf{7m 6cm}$$

2

Second glide	Naomi	Kris	Gordon	Marie	Rashmi
	3m 46cm	4m 12cm	3m 5cm	2m 99cm	400cm

(a) Calculate the **total** of the **two** glide lengths for each child.

(b) The winner has the longest total glide length.
Name the winner and the next two children in order.

In another game, the children dive for a weight.

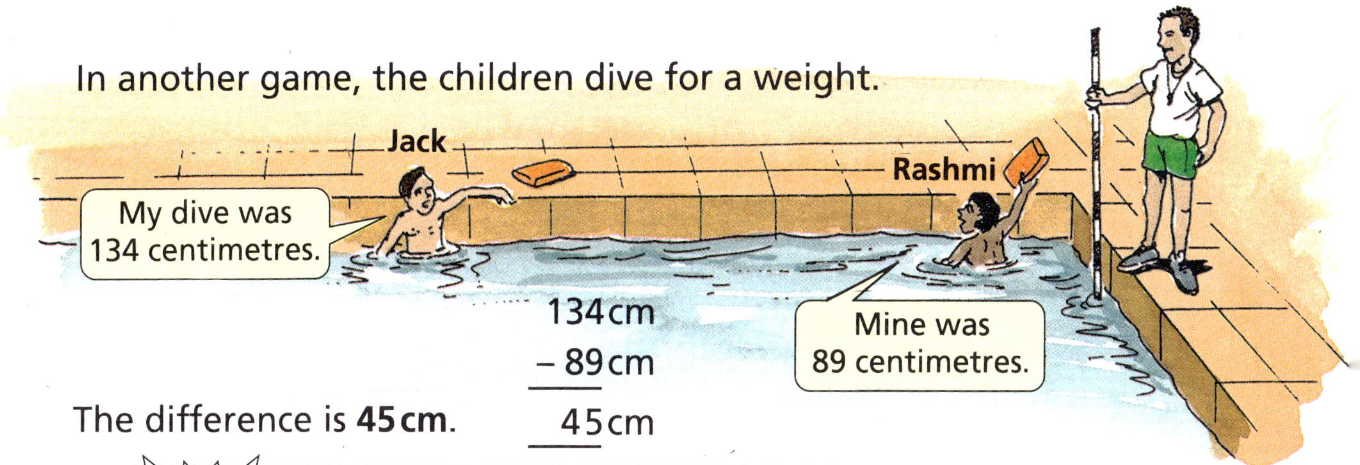

$$\begin{array}{r} 134\text{cm} \\ -\ 89\text{cm} \\ \hline 45\text{cm} \end{array}$$

The difference is **45cm**.

3

Dive depths	Naomi	Kris	Gordon	Marie	Jan
	1m 73cm	205cm	2m 14cm	123cm	2m

Find the **difference** in depth between

(a) Rashmi's dive and each of the others' dives

(b) the deepest dive and each of the others.

71 In at the deep end

Length: tenths of a metre

1 Look at this drawing of a metre stick. 

(a) How many coloured strips does it have?

(b) What **fraction** of one metre is each coloured strip?

2 Use a metre stick or a long tape marked in tenths of a metre. Measure some objects to the **nearest tenth of a metre**. Record the lengths like this:

height of bench ⟶ about $\frac{3}{10}$ m
width of door ⟶ about

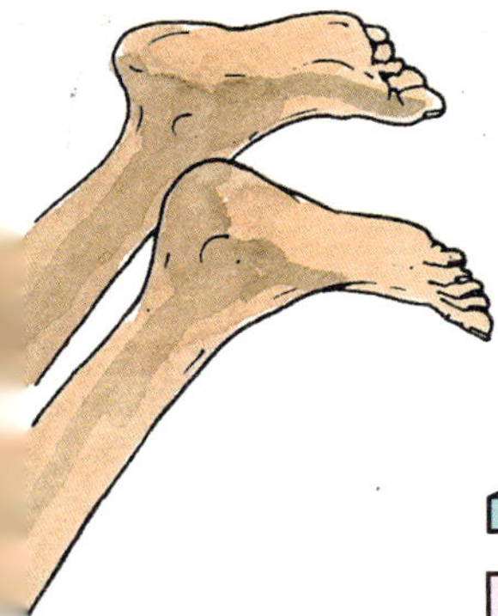

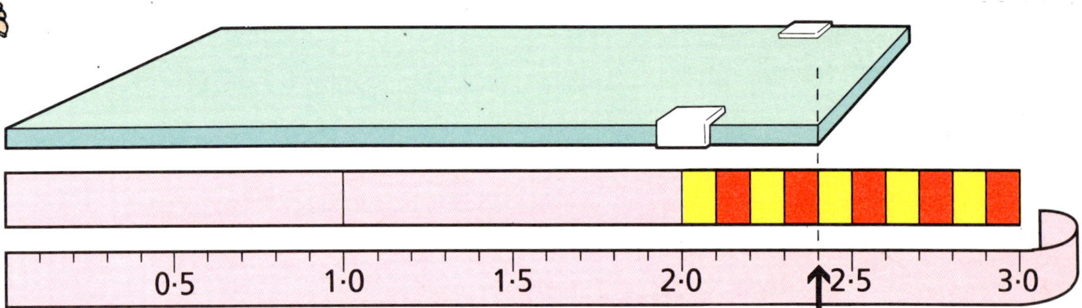

The length of the diving board is **$2\frac{4}{10}$** m
$2\frac{4}{10}$ m written in decimal form is **2·4** m

3 Write the lengths you measured in question **2** in decimal form.

Problem solving

4 The edges of the square tiles on the swimming pool walls are each 0·1 metres long.

(a) What is the perimeter of the **rectangle** made from

2 tiles  3 tiles?

(b) How many tiles are there in a row which makes a rectangle with a perimeter of 1·6 metres?

Ask your teacher what to do next.

Junior Rangers

Dan is in charge of the Junior Ranger Club at Atholl Wood.

1 Find each area in square centimetres.

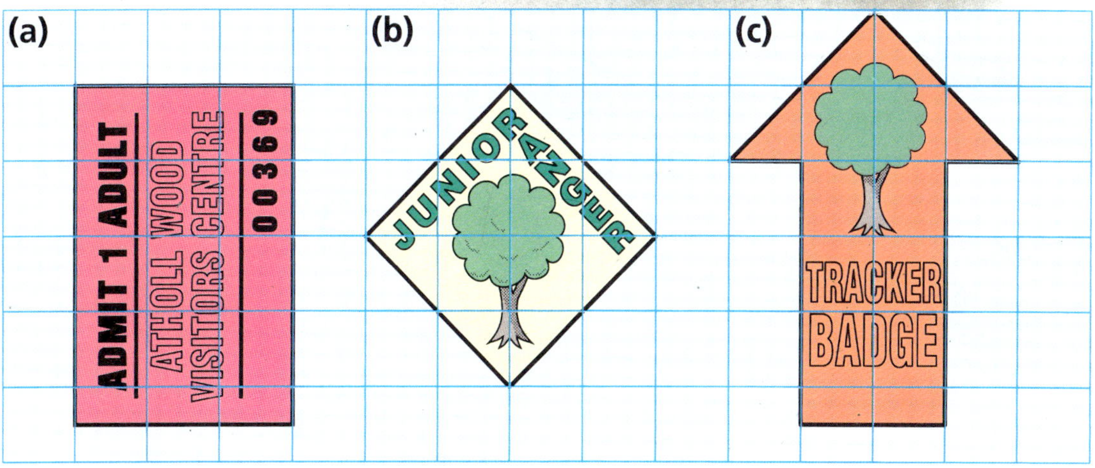

You need centimetre squared paper.

2 Help the Junior Rangers by designing

Problem solving

- **(a)** your own badge and finding its area
- **(b)** a **square** badge with an area of 36 cm^2
- **(c)** a **rectangular** badge of area $22\frac{1}{2}$ cm^2.

3 Dan made a **square** badge using **four** of these shapes.

Problem solving

- **(a)** What is the area of this shape?
- **(b)** Make four copies of the shape on centimetre squared paper.
- **(c)** Make each copy a different colour.
- **(d)** Cut out the 4 shapes. Fit them together to make a square.
- **(e)** What is the area of Dan's square badge?

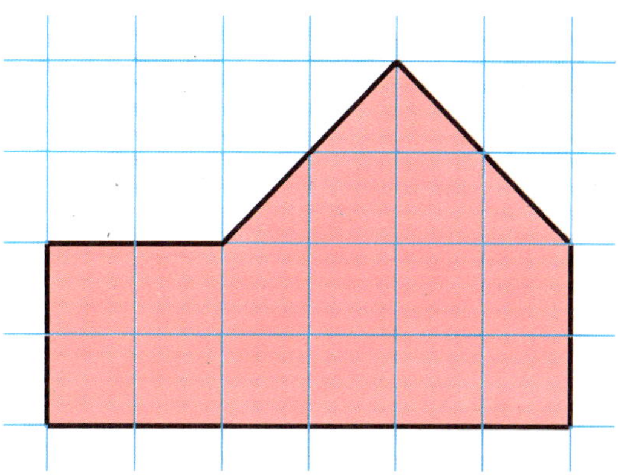

Go to Workbook page 27.

Carol's Carpets

Work as a group. You need metre sticks, large sheets of paper, and sticky tape.

1 Carol sells square carpet tiles with sides 50 cm long.
Use paper to make **one** carpet tile like this:

2 **(a)** Does your paper tile completely cover the surface of your desk?

(b) Make 20 of these tiles altogether.

3 **(a)** Join 4 tiles to make a larger square like this:
Keep the rest of your tiles for page 74.

(b) What length is each side of this square?

Your large paper square has an area of about **1 square metre.**

4 How many of each of these fit into your square metre:

(a) children **(b)** maths textbooks **(c)** sheets of paper?

5 Name a surface in your classroom which you estimate has

(a) an area **greater than** 1 square metre

(b) an area **smaller than** 1 square metre

(c) an area of **about** 1 square metre.

Check your estimates.

6 Use your paper carpet tiles.

(a) **Lay out** 4 tiles to make each of these shapes. What is the area of each shape?

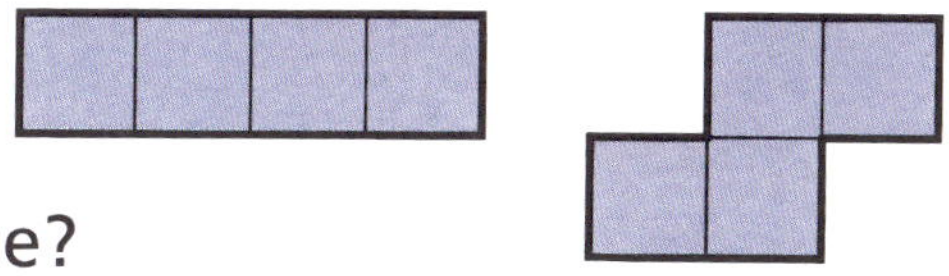

(b) Make two other different shapes with an area of 4 tiles.

7 Join tiles like this to make a supply of square metres.

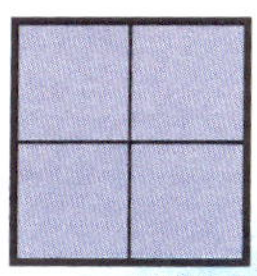

Work with a partner.

Problem solving

8 (a) Carol wants a new carpet for her office. The floor is a rectangle with length 4 m and breadth 3 m. Use your paper square metres to find the area of carpet she needs.

1 square metre can be written **$1\,m^2$**

(b) Carol is going to paint one wall in her office. The wall is a rectangle with length 4 m and height 2 m. Does the tin contain enough paint for this? Explain.

Ask your teacher what to do next.

The Kluless laboratory

Professor Kluless is showing his assistant Zantha how to weigh using 20g, 10g and 5g weights.

1 Find an object which weighs

(a) about 20 grams **(b)** about 10 grams **(c)** about 5 grams.

2 The items in the store have no labels. Zantha weighed each one in grams. What does each contain?

(a)

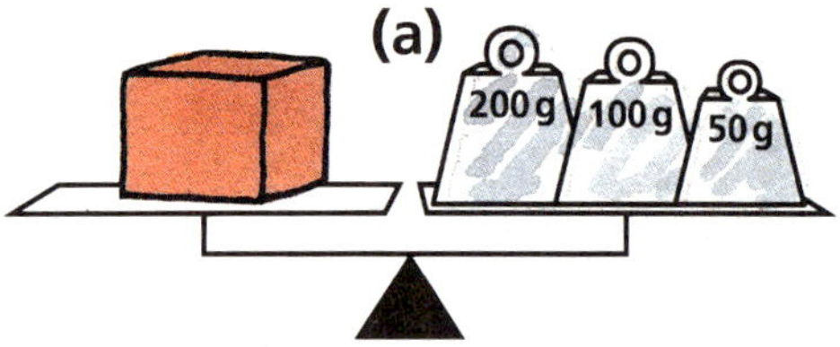

(b)

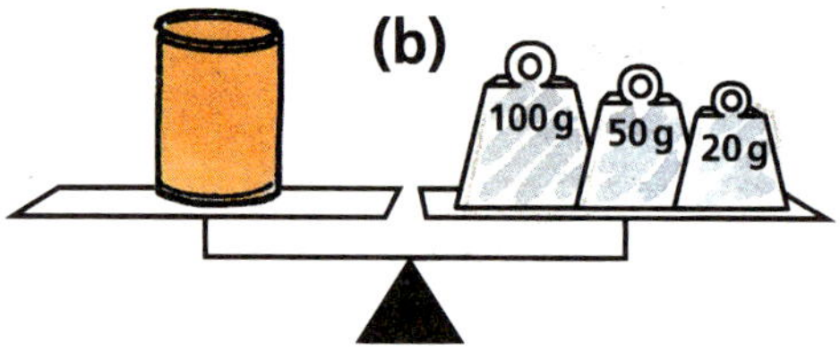

(c)

(d)

(e)

(f)

3 Zantha has this set of weights. List the weights she should use to weigh each jar of ooze.

You need a balance, weights and parcels A, B, C, D and E.

1 Take a 100 g weight in your hand.
Estimate which parcels weigh
(a) less than 100 g **(b)** more than 100 g.

2 Use the balance. Find the weight of each of the parcels A, B, C, D and E.

3 Zantha is weighing grime and gunge.
Copy and complete her notes:

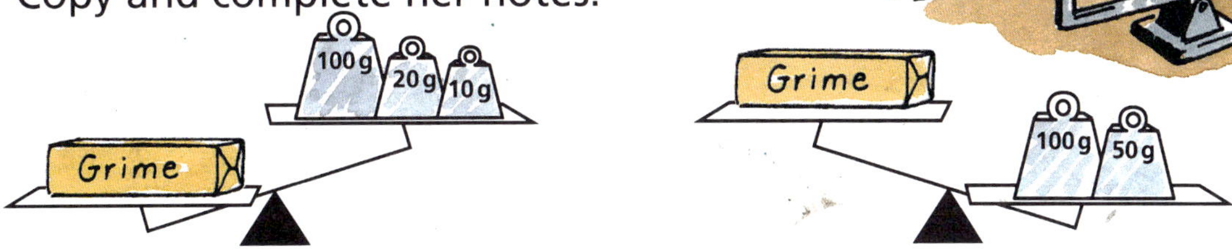

(a) Weight of grime: between ____ g and ____ g

(b) Weight of gunge: between ____ g and ____ g

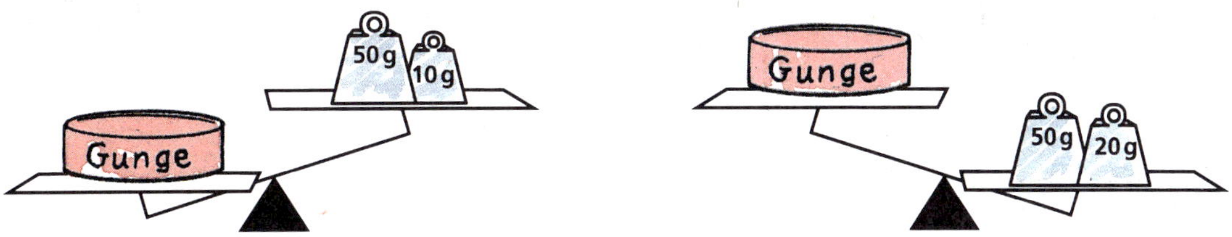

4 Find the weights of about 6 different objects.

5 Look at these balances. Help Zantha find the weight of **one** box of fungus.

Problem solving

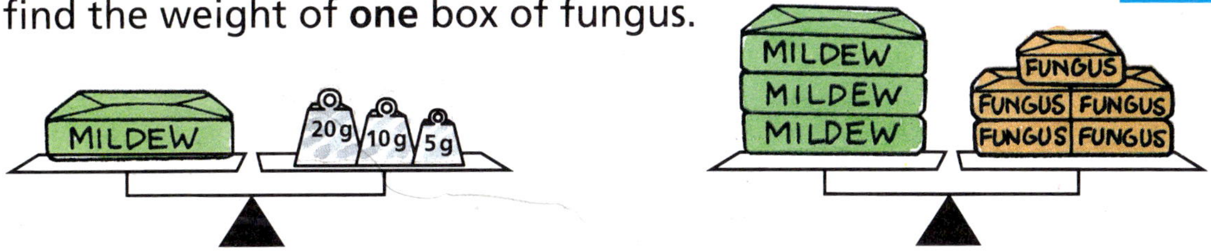

The pickling room

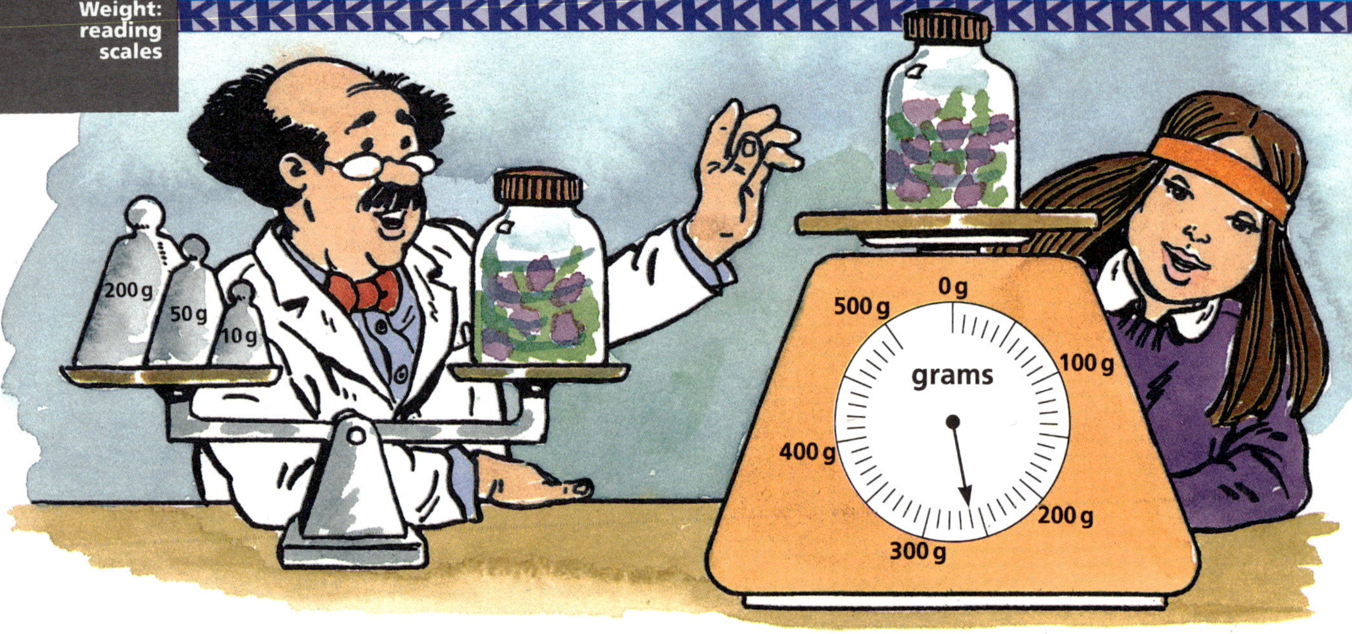

1 What is the weight shown on
(a) the Professor's balance **(b)** Zantha's scale?

2 This is the Professor's recipe for *Pickled thistles.*

Read the scales to find the weight of each ingredient.

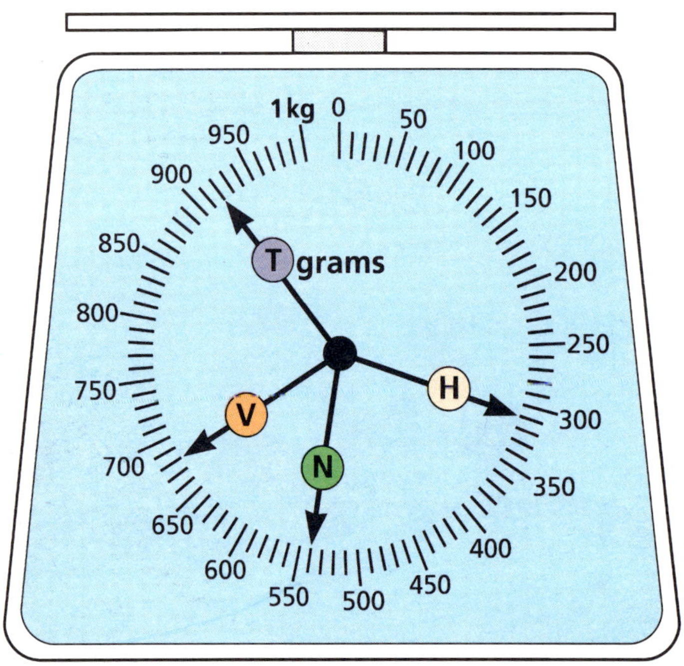

Pickled thistles

- (H) honey
- (N) nettles
- (V) vinegar
- (T) thistle heads
- (S) salt
- (C) chilli
- (D) dandelion
- (X) factor *X*

Mix well. Cover and leave for 2 weeks.

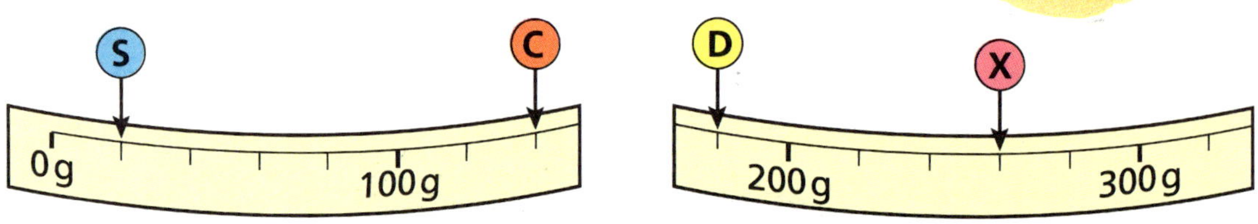

1 Find the weights of these ingredients.

H hops
E elderflowers
W watercress
G garlic
M marigold
S spearmint
B basil

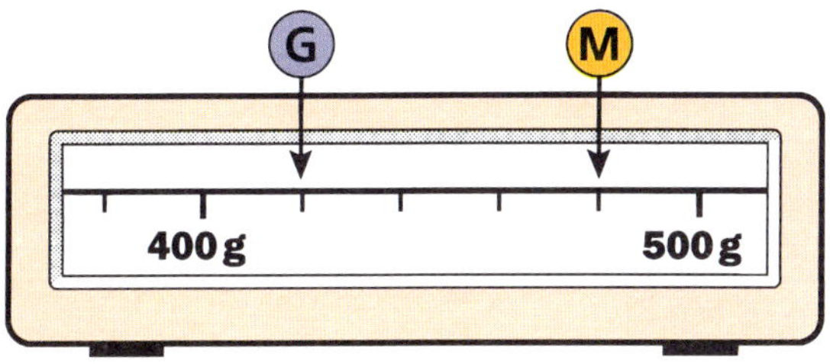

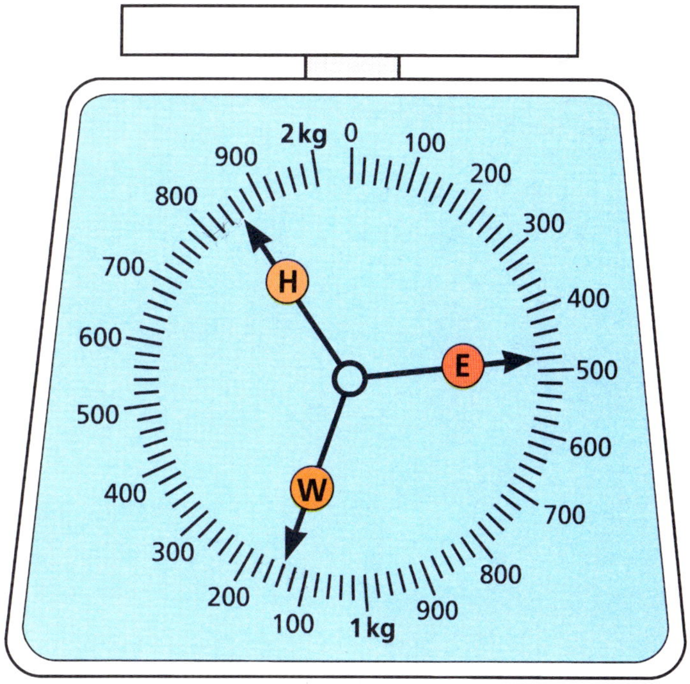

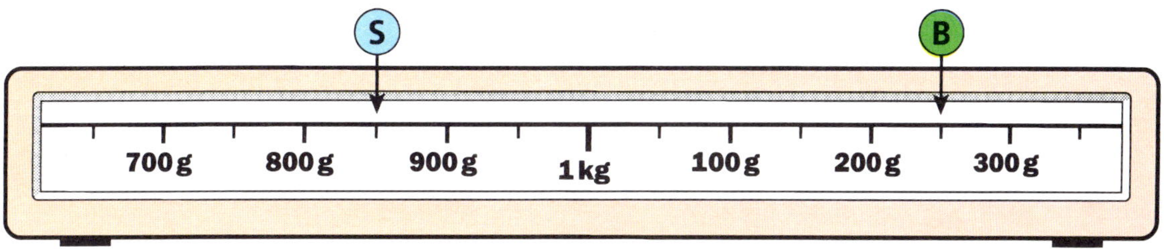

2 Ask your teacher for 4 boxes from the pickling room.
Use scales to find the weight of each box.

3 Make up this parcel for Professor Kluless.

Problem solving

To *Professor Kluless* **Date** *20th June*

Please send one of your mystery parcels. It must contain 4 items. The weight of the parcel should be between 1 kg 600 g and 1 kg 800 g.

From *Comfrey Health Stores*

Go to Workbook page 29.

Ask your teacher if you can make Zantha's Special Fudge.

Zantha's Special Fudge

200g biscuits
100g butter
2 level tablespoons syrup
2 level tablespoons sugar
1 level tablespoon cocoa

Crush the biscuits.
Add the cocoa.
Melt the butter, syrup and sugar.
Mix everything together.
Press into a tin to make the base.

200g icing sugar
$1\frac{1}{2}$ tablespoons water
$\frac{1}{2}$ teaspoon factor X

Mix together.
Spread on top of base.
Melt **150 grams of chocolate.**
Spread over.

Ask your teacher what to do next.

The Green Hut Gang

1 The gang are looking for things to do during their school holidays. Write each time using **past** and **to**.

(a) They start at
35 minutes past 9
25 minutes to 10

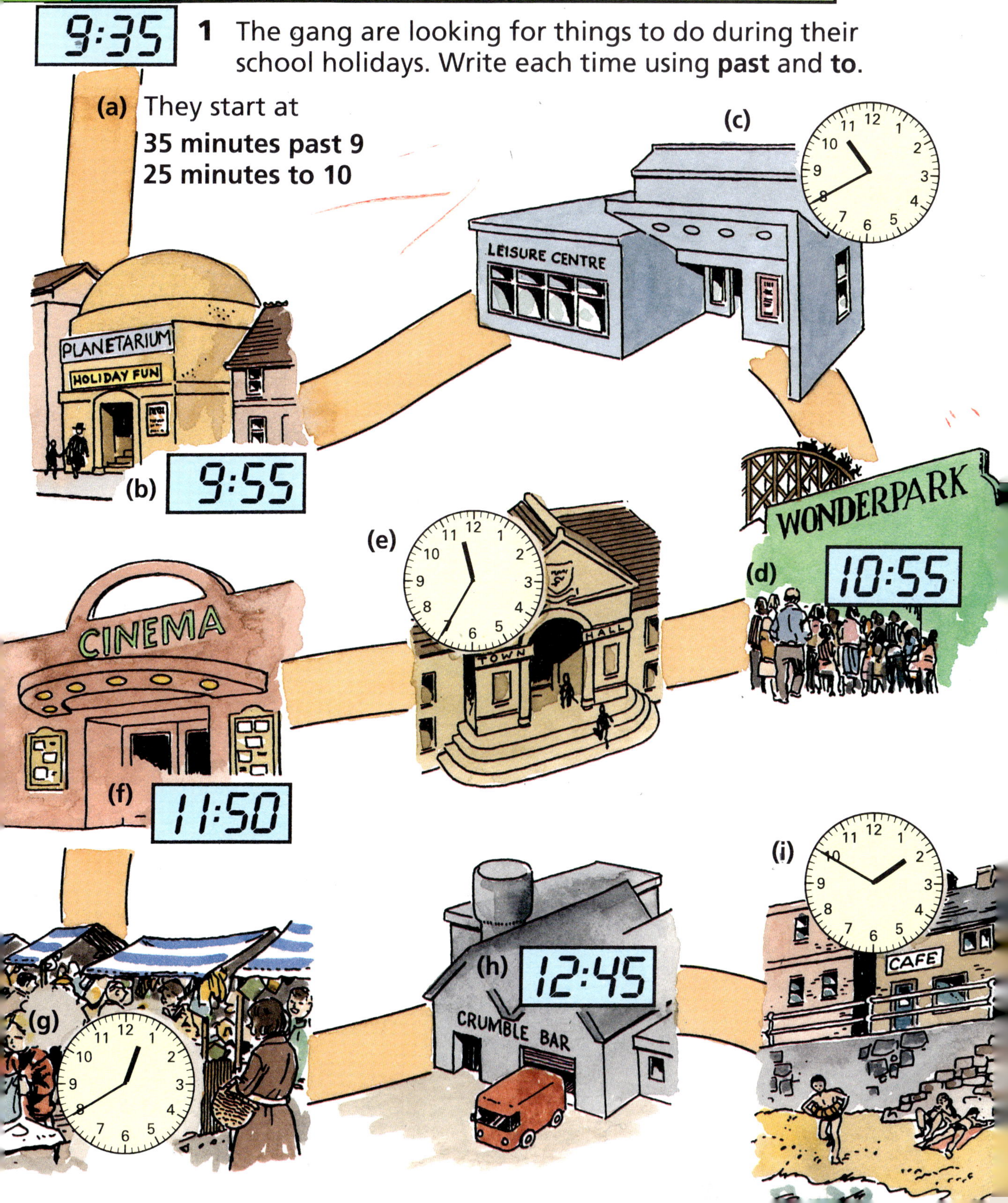

At the cinema

1 *Planet Z* starts **just before** 20 to 4. Write the times when the other films start using **just before** or **just after**.

2 *Planet Z* starts at **39 minutes past 3**. Write the times for the other films in this way.

3 Write the time each cartoon starts like this: *Mighty Dino*: 23 minutes to 4

4 The clocks show when each child left the cinema. Write the times using past **or** to.

(a) Mandy **(b)** Glen **(c)** Karim **(d)** Tessa

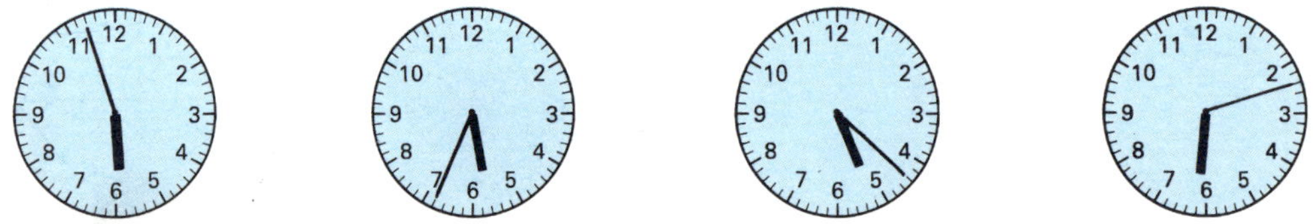

Crumble Bar factory

82

Time: to the nearest minute

Roz and Matt visit the factory where their Dad works.

1 **(a)** Write the time for each event using past **or** to:

wrapping 23 minutes past 2

(b) List the events **in order**.

2 Use **past** to write the time when each person leaves the factory.

(a) the packer

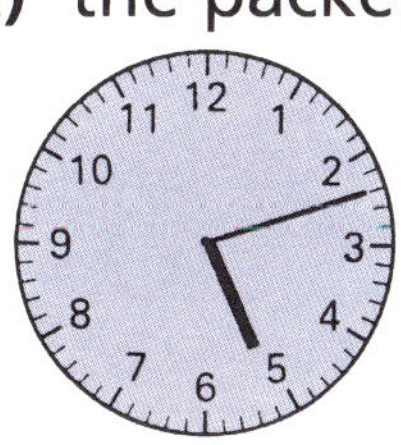

(b) the manager

(c) the cleaner

At the beach

The beach clock shows 25 to 9
or 35 minutes past 8.
This is written as 8.35

Beach shop hours
(except Thursday)

1 In the same way, write the times when the beach shop
(a) opens in the morning
(b) closes for lunch
(c) opens in the afternoon
(d) closes in the evening.

2 Each Thursday the shop opens one hour later in the morning and closes two hours earlier in the evening.
Write the **Thursday** times.

Mandy's diary shows what the gang did during the morning.

Tuesday

Today we went to the beach.

	arrived	left
café	8.30	9.15
shop	9.20	10.05
swimming pool	10.40	12.15
snack bar	12.35	2.00

3 Write in words the times when the children
(a) arrived at the café
(b) left the shop
(c) arrived at the pool
(d) left the snack bar.

4 Where were the children at
(a) 5 to 10
(b) 20 past 11
(c) quarter to 9
(d) quarter past 1
(e) 9.00
(f) 1.55
(g) 9.30
(h) noon?

opens	Beach Car Park	closes
8.30 am		8.30 pm

For times before 12 noon, we write am.
For times after 12 noon, we write pm.

TALENT COMPETITIONS

beautiful baby	9.50 am
best singer	11.00 am
best dancer	12.05 pm
best comic	1.35 pm
best acrobat	4.15 pm
star lookalike	7.45 pm

1 Which talent competitions are held
(a) in the morning
(b) in the afternoon or evening?

2 Mandy arrived at 12.10 pm.
Which competition was taking place at this time?

Boat trips to Seal Island

Departure times: 11.00 11.40 12.20 1.00 1.40 2.20
Evening cruises: 6.50 7.30

3 **(a)** Write the boat departure times, using am or pm.
(b) The gang arrived too late for the first afternoon sailing. Which departure times were still available?

4 Write the times for the pony rides using am or pm.

pony rides from 9.15 am and every hour until 3.15 pm

Problem solving

Puppet show	Benny the clown	Sports	
11.00 am – 1.15 pm	3 shows daily	sack race	11.40 am
2.15 pm – 4.00 pm	12 noon till 12.30 pm	egg and spoon race	12.00
	1.00 pm till 1.30 pm	obstacle race	12.20 pm
	2.00 pm till 2.30 pm		

5 In the **afternoon** the gang saw the Puppet show and Benny the clown, and took part in some races. Make up their afternoon timetable.

Leisure centre

Time: durations in minutes

1 The gang visit the gym first.
How many minutes does each person spend in the gym?

	start		finish
(a) Glen	2:00	→	2:15
(b) Karim	2:10	→	2:25
(c) Mandy	2:15	→	2:40
(d) Matt	2:05	→	2:45
(e) Roz	2:25	→	2:50
(f) Tessa	2:30	→	2:55

They agree to meet in the Badminton Hall at 3.00 pm.
At 2.25 Karim works out that there are
35 minutes until 3.00 pm.

2 How many minutes are there from each time until 3.00 pm?

Roz
2.50

Glen
2.15

Mandy
2.40

Matt
2.45

Tessa starts playing at 3.50 pm. She stops playing at 4.15 pm.

← From 3.50 to 4.00 is 10 minutes.

From 4.00 to 4.15 is 15 minutes. →

Tessa plays for **25 minutes**.

3 For how many minutes does each person play?

(a) Glen

(b) Karim

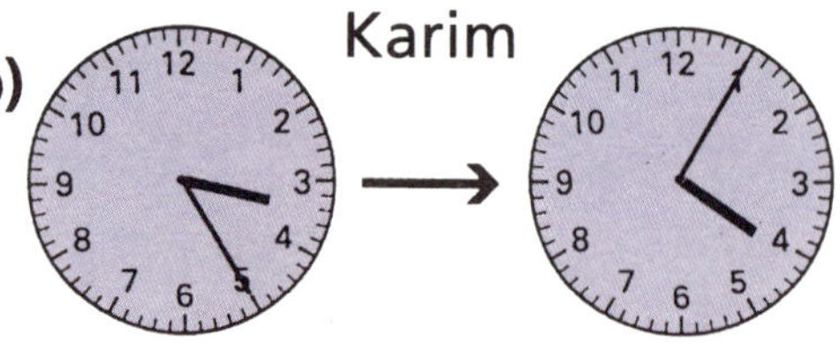

(c) Mandy

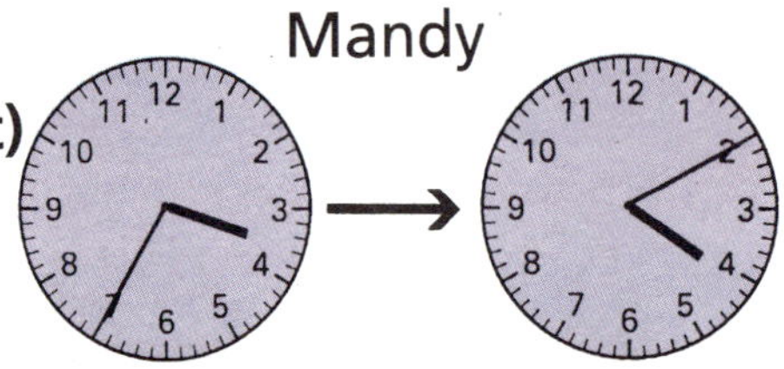

(d) Roz

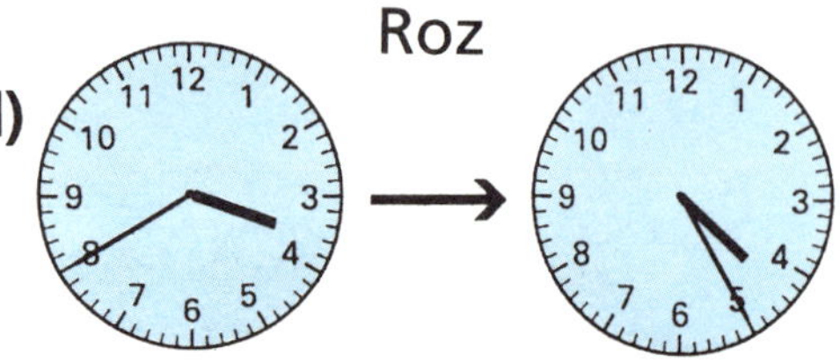

(e) Matt: 3.55 to 4.35

(f) Matt's friend: 3.50 to 4.40

1 How many hours does each of the six classes last?

Roz works out how long a beginner's swimming lesson lasts.

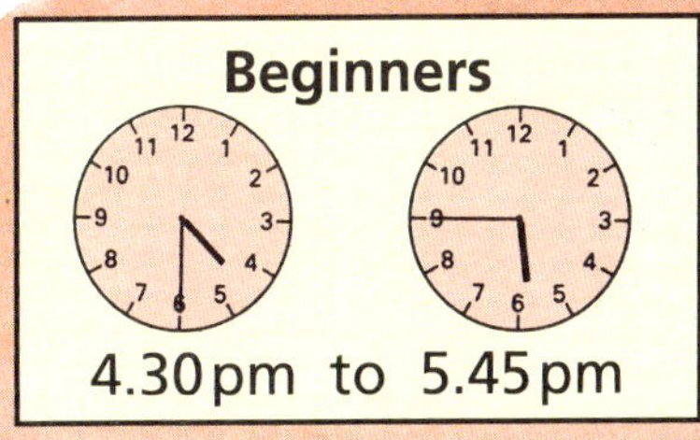

The lesson lasts for **1 hour 15 minutes**.

2 For how long does the attendant supervise each activity?

(a) *Flumes*:

6.00 pm to 7.20 pm

(b) *Turkish baths*: 10.05 am – 11.10 am
(c) *Diving pool*: 3.20 pm – 5.50 pm
(d) *Sauna*: 11.15 am – 12.45 pm
(e) *Learners' pool*: 1.35 pm – 3.00 pm

3 How long does each person take to travel home?

		leaves centre	arrives home
(a)	Karim	5.20 pm	6.30 pm
(b)	Mandy	5.35 pm	6.50 pm
(c)	Glen	5.40 pm	6.45 pm
(d)	Matt	5.45 pm	6.10 pm
(e)	Roz	6.05 pm	7.15 pm
(f)	Tessa	6.15 pm	7.30 pm

4 Glen watches TV until 'Star Tour' ends at 8.15 pm. How long does each programme last?

87 Computer games

Time: durations, counting on

The gang plan to play computer games at Glen's house.

If we start at 4.30 pm and play for 2 hours
4.30 . . . 5.30 . . . 6.30
we will finish at **6.30 pm**.

1 Find the finishing times.

	start at	play for
(a)	5 pm	3 hours
(b)	11 am	2 hours
(c)	2.30 pm	1 hour
(d)	10.30 am	3 hours

	start at	play for
(e)	12.15 pm	1 hour
(f)	3.45 pm	2 hours
(g)	11.20 am	3 hours
(h)	6.40 pm	2 hours

The computer game *Treasure* has a time limit.
The screen blanks out after **15 minutes'** play.

Mandy starts at 4.40 pm.
The screen blanks out at **4.55 pm**.

2 When does the screen blank out for these players?

		starts at			starts at
(a)	Karim	3.30 pm	**(b)**	Roz	10.35 am
(c)	Glen	6.05 pm	**(d)**	Tessa	12.45 pm

Glen and Mandy are playing *Star-trooper*.
They start at 5.30 pm and play for 45 minutes.

← 5.30 pm and **30 minutes** is 6.00 pm.
6.00 pm and **15 minutes** is 6.15 pm. →

They finish at **6.15pm**.

3 Find the finishing times for each person for each game.

	(a) Karim starts at	(a) Karim plays for	(b) Roz starts at	(b) Roz plays for
Star-trooper	4.45 pm	20 minutes	11.15 am	55 minutes
Lost Princess	5.20 pm	50 minutes	2.35 pm	30 minutes
Jungle Drum	9.50 am	25 minutes	12.25 pm	45 minutes

1 Next day Karim hires a new game called *Robot*. Everyone wants to play it, so he makes a timetable. Find the starting time for each player.

Player	starts at	plays for	finishes at
Tessa		1 hour	10.00 am
Matt		1 hour	11.30 am
Mandy		2 hours	1.45 pm
Roz		2 hours	3.50 pm
Glen		3 hours	7.15 pm

Tessa plays *Treasure 2* with a time limit of **25 minutes**. After the screen blanks out she sees this message. →

She works out that she started playing at **7.10 pm**

2 Find the starting times.

	Player	Time limit	stopped
(a)	Mandy	25 minutes	6.30 pm
(b)	Matt	25 minutes	4.45 pm

	Player	Time limit	stopped
(c)	Karim	25 minutes	2.40 pm
(d)	Roz	25 minutes	12.50 pm

Glen found the *Lost Princess* at 8.15 pm after playing for 45 minutes. When did he start?

← From 8.15 go back **15 minutes** to 8.00.
From 8.00 go back **30 minutes** to 7.30 →

Glen started playing at **7.30 pm**.

3 Find the starting times.

(a) Mandy found the princess at 3.20 pm, after 30 minutes.

(b) Karim found her at 10.05 am, after 20 minutes.

(c) Tessa found her at 2.35 pm, after 40 minutes.

(d) Roz found her at 5.10 pm, after 25 minutes.

Go to Workbook page 7.

Green Hut calendar

May

Sun	Mon	Tue	Wed	Thu	Fri	Sat
			1 Computer Club	2	3 Drama Club	4
5	6 Holiday	7 Mandy's birthday	8 Computer Club	9	10	11
12	13	14	15 Computer Club	16 Glen's birthday	17 Drama Club	18
19	20	21 Karim's birthday	22 Computer Club	23	24	25
26	27 Holiday	28	29 Computer Club	30	31 Drama Club	

Use the gang's calendar.

1 Write the day of the week for these dates:

(a) 1st May **(b)** 10th May **(c)** 18th May **(d)** 25th May.

2 Mandy's birthday is **Tuesday 7th May**.
Write the dates for Karim's and Glen's birthdays.

3 The gang go swimming every Saturday in May.
Write the dates of these Saturdays.

4 How many **weeks** are there between

(a) Computer Club meetings **(b)** Drama Club meetings

(c) Mandy's and Karim's birthdays **(d)** the two holidays?

5 Tessa's mum's birthday is 30th April. Her father's is 1st June.
Write the days of the week for these dates.

6 Roz and Matt's date of birth is 9th January 1987.
This can be written as 9.1.87 or 9/1/87 or 09–01–87.
Write these dates of birth in one of these ways:

(a) Roz's dad: third of October nineteen fifty-two

(b) Tessa: twenty-fifth of August nineteen eighty-five.

7 **Use this year's calendar.** Find the days of the week for all six gang members' birthdays.

Holidays

July

Sun	Mon	Tue	Wed	Thu	Fri	Sat
	1	2	3	4	5	6
7	8	9	10	11	12	13
14	15	16	17	18	19	20
21	22	23	24	25	26	27
28	29	30	31			

August

Sun	Mon	Tue	Wed	Thu	Fri	Sat
				1	2	3
4	5	6	7	8	9	10
11	12	13	14	15	16	17
18	19	20	21	22	23	24
25	26	27	28	29	30	31

1 Here are the gang members' holiday dates.
For how many weeks is each person on holiday?

(a) Karim : 7th July to 21st July
(b) Tessa : 2nd July to 23rd July
(c) Mandy : 24th July to 14th August
(d) Glen : 30th July to 13th August

2 Roz and Matt go on holiday on 16th August for 2 weeks. Write the date they return.

3 Look at the numbers in the red column.
Look at the numbers in another column.
What do you notice about each number sequence?

4 The first Wednesday in December is the 4th.
Write the dates of the other Wednesdays in December.

5 Write the date two weeks after 12th October.

6 Matt makes a holiday timetable.

14 days before	7 days before	Start of holiday	7 days after	14 days after
(a) buy clothes	**(b)** buy film	Saturday 17th August	**(c)** hire bike	**(d)** send postcards

Write the day and date for each event on Matt's timetable.

Ask your teacher what to do next.

91 Calendar squares

Other activity: number squares

JUNE

Mon	Tue	Wed	Thu	Fri	Sat	Sun
		1	2	3	4	5
6	7	8	9	10	11	12
13	14	15	16	17	18	19
20	21	22	23	24	25	26
27	28	29	30			

JULY

Mon	Tue	Wed	Thu	Fri	Sat	Sun
				1	2	3
4	5	6	7	8	9	10
11	12	13	14	15	16	17
18	19	20	21	22	23	24
25	26	27	28	29	30	31

1 Sam has coloured a 2 by 2 square on the June calendar.

(a) Find the total of the four numbers in the square.

(b) This is Sam's method for finding this total. Does his method work for other 2 by 2 squares on the June calendar?

Sam's method

Take smallest number. 15
Add 4. + 4
19

Multiply by 4. × 4
Total 76

2 Samantha has coloured a 3 by 3 square on the July calendar.

I can find the total of nine numbers.

Samantha's method

Take the smallest number.
Add 8.
Multiply the answer by 9.

(a) Does her method work?

(b) Try this for other 3 by 3 squares on the July and June calendars.

3 Work with a partner.

Try to discover **other** ways of finding the total of

(a) nine numbers in a 3 by 3 calendar square

(b) four numbers in a 2 by 2 square.

All mixed up

1 Professor Kluless has $\frac{1}{4}$ **litre** of Juniper juice. What volume does he have in each of the other bottles?

Work with a partner.

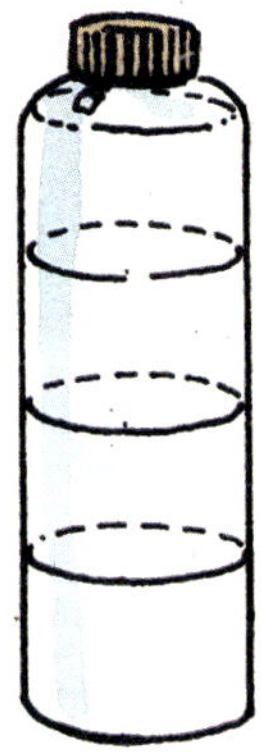

2 Make a measuring bottle. You need
- a large plastic bottle
- 1 litre, $\frac{1}{2}$ l and $\frac{1}{4}$ l measures
- a funnel
- elastic bands or a marker pen.

Mark the levels for $\frac{1}{4}$ l, $\frac{1}{2}$ l, $\frac{3}{4}$ l and 1 l.

3 **(a)** Find containers which you **estimate** have a volume of
- about $\frac{1}{4}$ litre
- about $\frac{3}{4}$ l.

(b) Check using your measuring bottle.

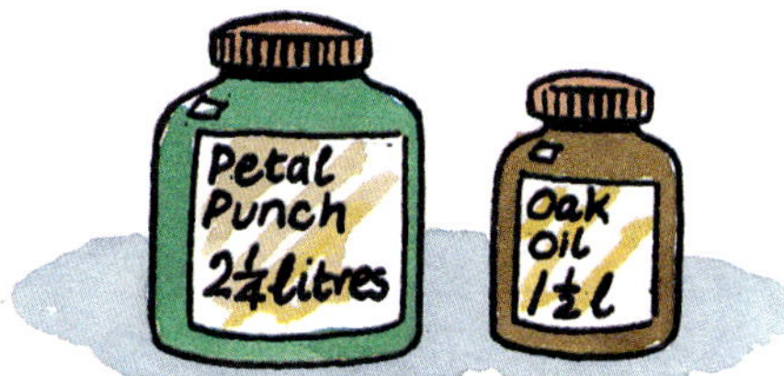

4 How many $\frac{1}{4}$ l measures can be filled from the bottle of

(a) Petal punch **(b)** Oak oil?

Problem solving

5 The Professor uses 1 litre of Nettle nectar to make up this special drink.

(a) What volume of each of the other ingredients does he use?

(b) What is the **total volume** of the *Kluless Special*?

Computer units

Professor Kluless is fitting together units for his computer. Each unit has a volume of **1 cubic centimetre** or **1 cm^3**.

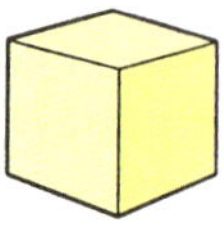

Use centimetre cubes.

1 Make each of these for Professor Kluless. Find the volume of each in cubic centimetres. Keep the shapes for question **2(b)**.

(a)

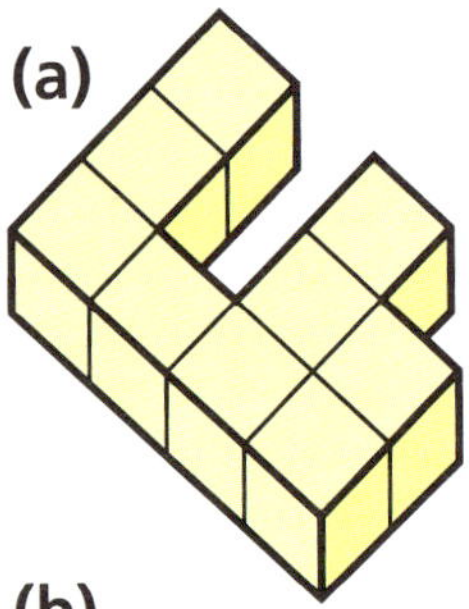

(b) (c) (d) (e) (f)

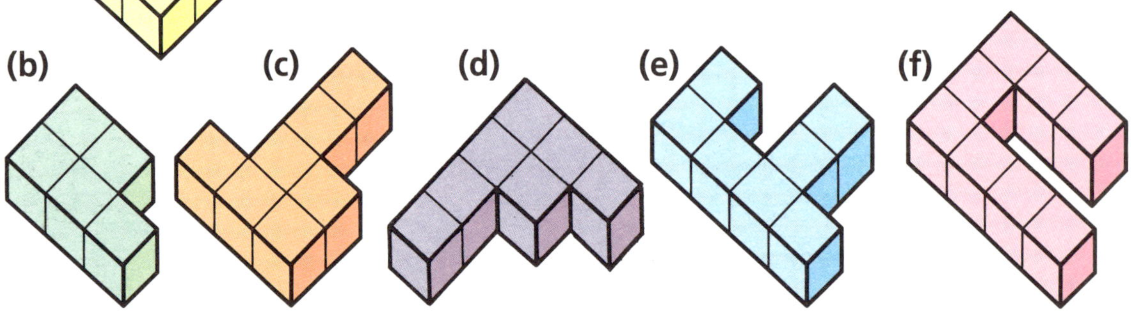

2 (a) What is the volume of each of these parts of the Professor's computer? Each unit is 1 cm^3.

Data Store | Thought Control | Memory

(b) Fit together **pairs** of the shapes from **question 1** to make these parts for the computer.

Problem solving

3 Make **six different** shapes, each with a volume of 4 cm^3.

Power packs

Professor Kluless uses small batteries, each with a volume of $1\,cm^3$.

Use centimetre cubes.

1 Find the volume of each set of batteries.

(a)

(b)

(c)

(d)

(e)

2 Zantha makes the batteries into power packs.
For each power pack, find

(a) the volume of batteries already in the pack

(b) the volume of batteries needed to fill the pack

(c) the total volume of the pack when full.

Super

Long life

Standard

Powerplus

Triple life

3 Make as many different power packs as you can.
Each one should be a **cuboid** with a volume of **$24\,cm^3$**.

Problem solving

Ask your teacher what to do next.

The stained-glass workshop

Alex makes stained-glass windows.

1 Copy each window design on squared paper.

2 Colour the designs so that each has the lines of symmetry shown.

(a)

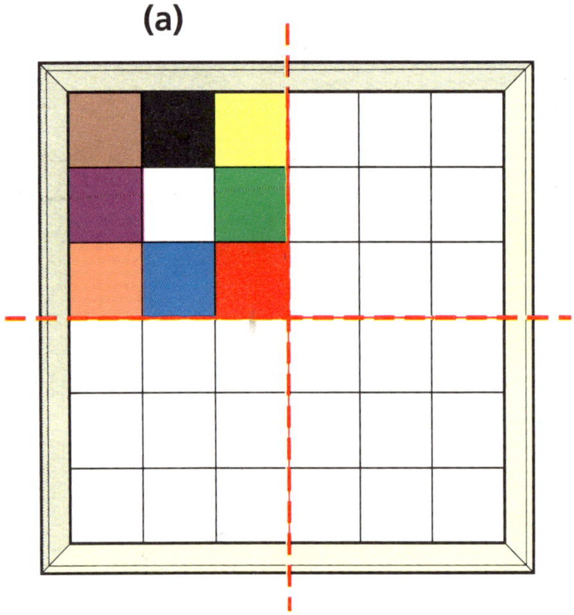

(b)

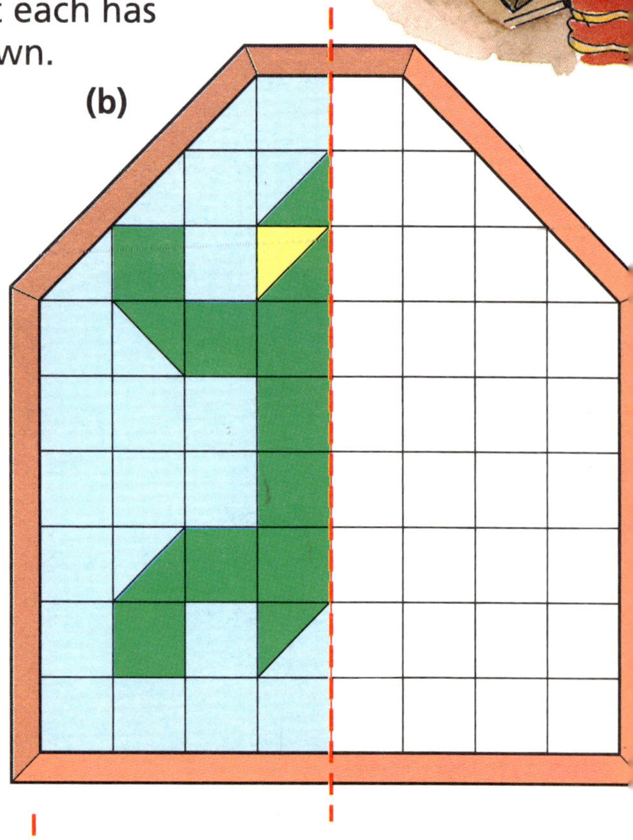

(c)

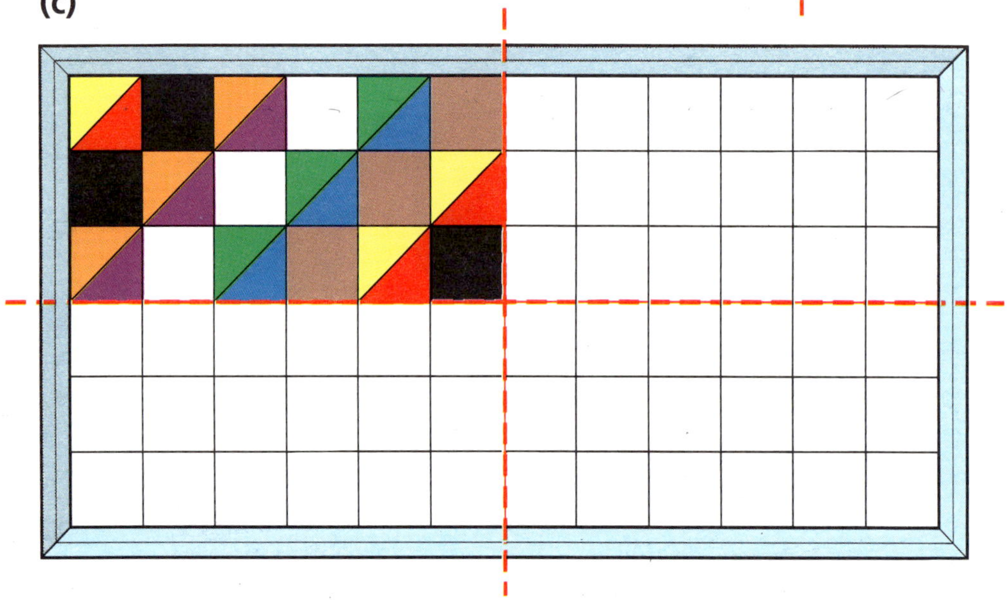

3 Draw and colour your own symmetrical window designs on squared paper.

In the frame

1 (a) Cut out the square from **Workbook page 18**.

(b) Fold it in half. →

(c) Open and draw the line of symmetry. →

(d) Fold and draw **all** its lines of symmetry.

(e) Write on the square its total number of lines of symmetry.

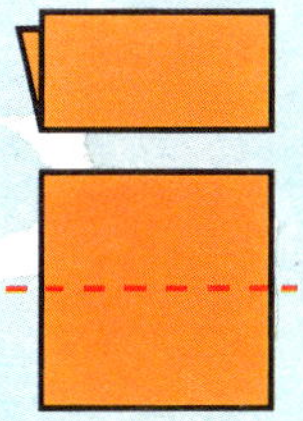

2 Do all this again for each shape on **Workbook page 18**.

3 Stick your shapes on paper to make a picture of a church.

4 **Use a paper circle.**
Design a pattern for a stained-glass window like this.

(a) Fold your paper circle to quarter it.

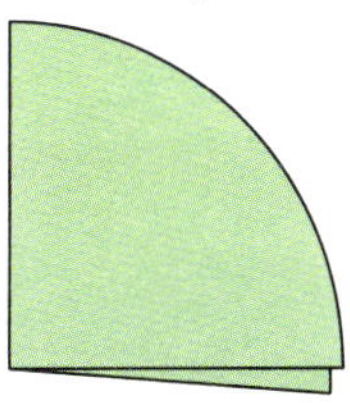

(b) Fold it again.

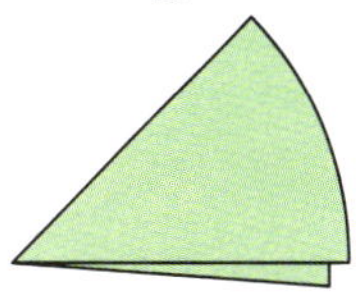

(c) Cut out some pieces.

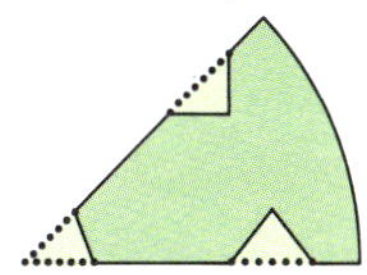

(d) Open the paper circle. Stick it in your exercise book. How many lines of symmetry does the design have?

5 Fold paper **squares** and cut out shapes to design patterns for square windows.

6 Here is Alex's design for a **circle** window.

Problem solving

(a) When opened out, how many holes do you **think** are made by the

- rectangle cut-outs
- curved cut-outs
- V-shaped cut-outs?

(b) Check by making the design.

Go to Workbook page 17.

Krazy kites

1 The kite which flew for the longest time has no lines of symmetry in its design. Which kite is this?

2 How many lines of symmetry has each of the other designs?

Ask your teacher what to do next.

Side by side

You need triangle paper and red, blue and green pencils.

1 Start in the middle.
Colour one triangle red.

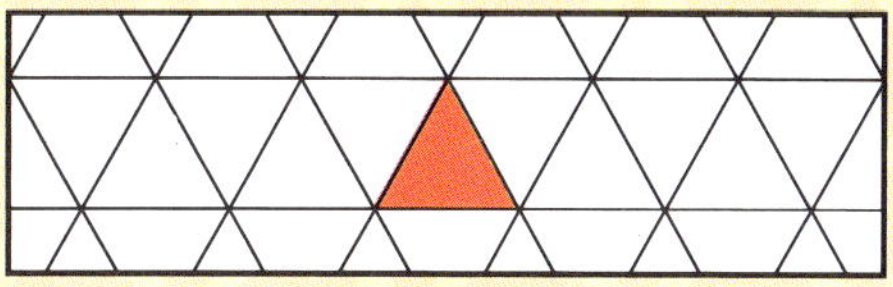

2 Colour blue, triangles which share a side with the red one.

3 Colour green, triangles which share a side with blue ones.

4 Colour red, triangles which share **only one** of their sides with green ones.

5 Colour blue, triangles which share **only one** of their sides with red ones.

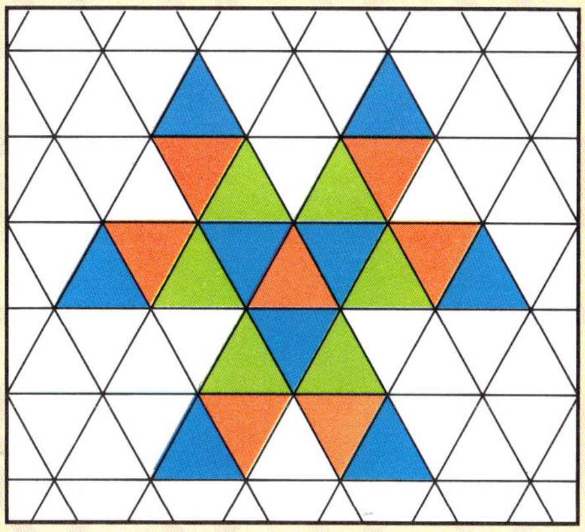

6 Continue the pattern.

99

3D shape: cubes, nets and skeleton models

A trinket box

1 Make a cube from a net using **one** of these two methods.

Method 1
Attach 6 **identical squares** together like this. →
Fold and tape to make a **cube**. Leave the lid of the box open.

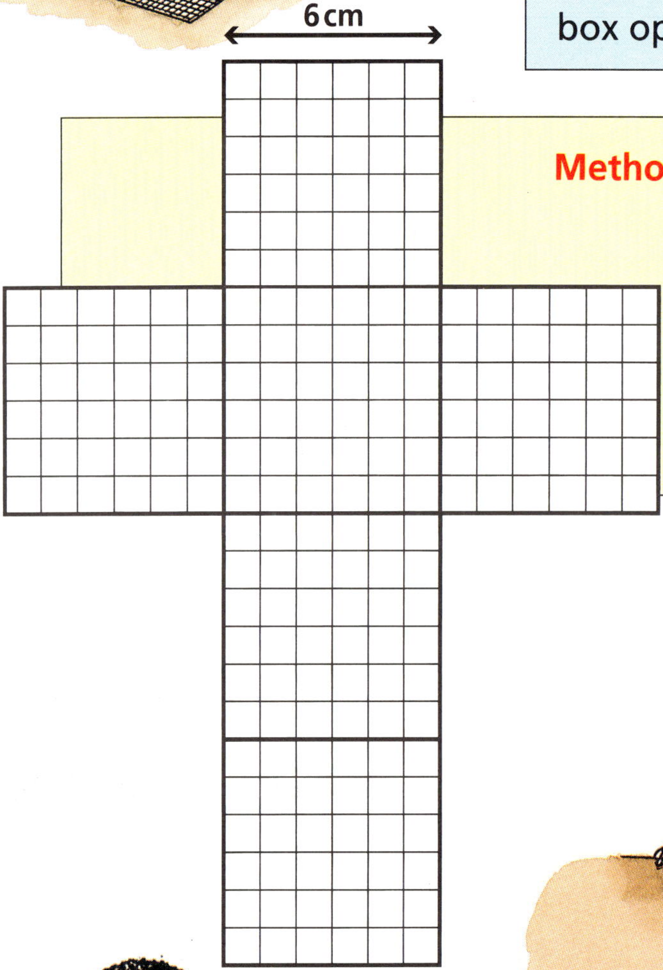

Method 2

- Draw a net like this on an A4 sheet of **centimetre** squared paper.
- Stick it on to card.
- Cut, fold and tape to make a **cube**, leaving the lid open.

2 Lyn made a cube with each edge 3 cm long.

(a) Draw a net for her cube on centimetre squared paper.

(b) Check that it makes a cube.

3 Ben made a skeleton cube using straws and plasticine.
Make a cube like this.

Nets of a cube

1 You need 6 identical squares and sticky tape.

(a) • Place the 6 squares like this.
• Tape the edges.
• Does this fold to make a cube?
If so, sketch this net on squared paper.

(b) Is this another net of a cube?

Work as a group.

(c) • Use 6 squares each time. Find as many other nets of a cube as you can.
• Each time you find one, sketch the net on squared paper.
• Make a chart.

Odds and ends

1 • Draw a net like this on an A4 sheet of **centimetre** squared paper.
• Stick it on to card.
• Cut, fold and tape to make a **cuboid**, leaving the lid open.
• Decorate the faces.

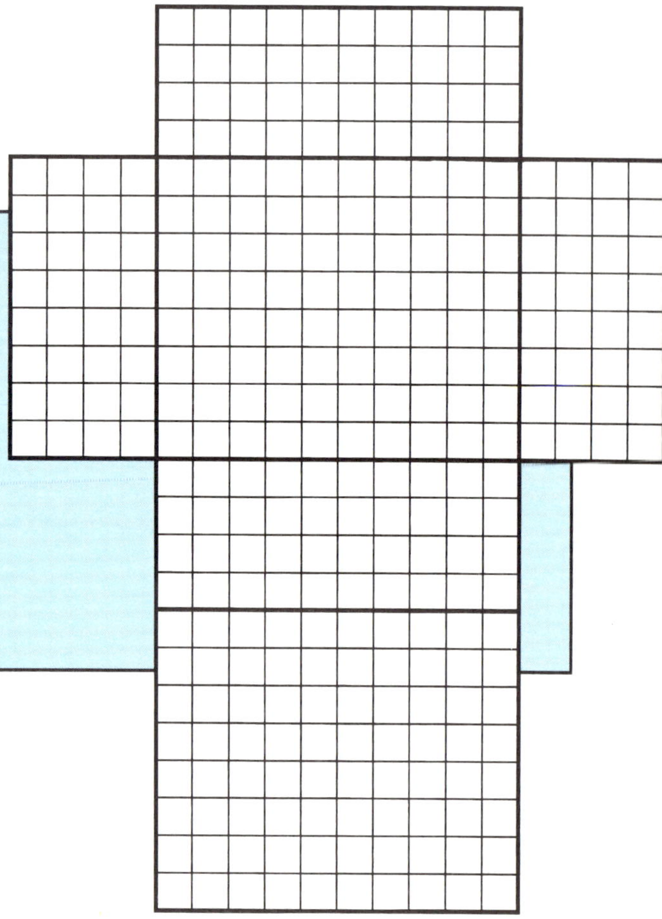

David used

4 rectangles like this ↓ **and** **2 squares** like this ↓ to make this cuboid. ↓

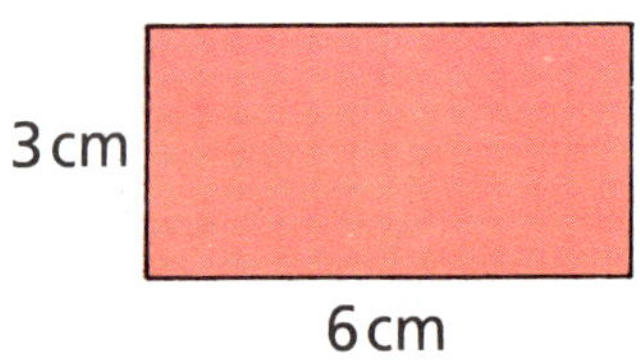

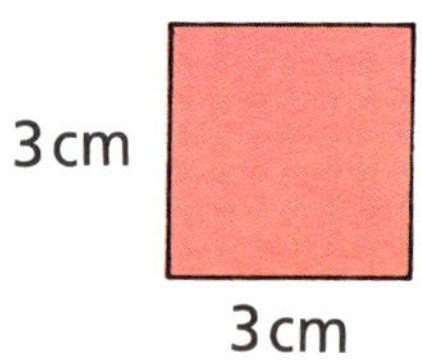

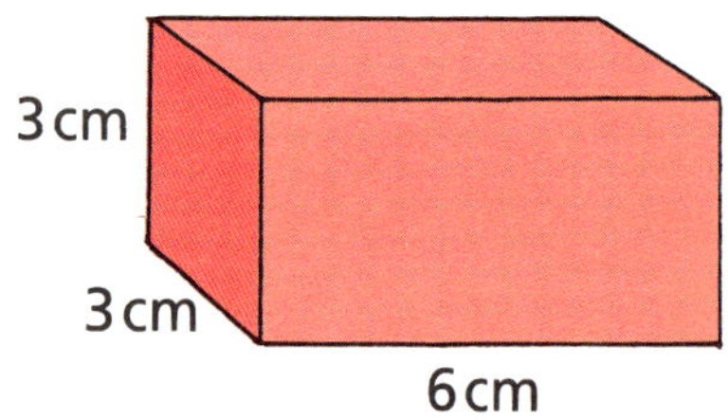

2 **(a)** Draw a net for this cuboid on centimetre squared paper.
(b) Check the net by folding.

3 Sally made a skeleton cuboid using straws and plasticine.

Make a cuboid like Sally's.

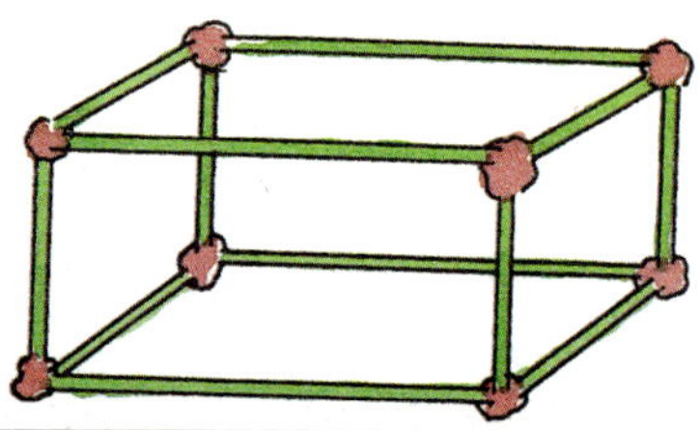

Ask your teacher what to do next.

Shapes from triangles

You need 6 identical triangles like this and triangle paper.

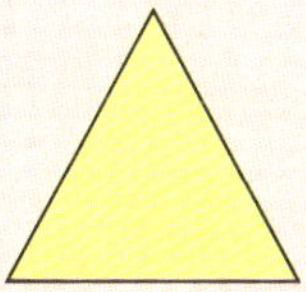

1 Use 4 triangles each time.

(a) Make each of these shapes.

(b) Draw each shape on your triangle paper.

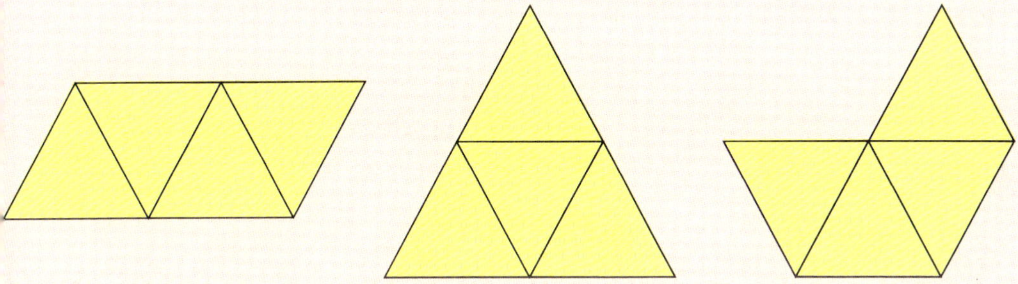

2 Make and draw all the different shapes you can,

(a) using 2 triangles (b) using 3 triangles

(c) using 5 triangles.

3 These two shapes are made using 6 triangles.

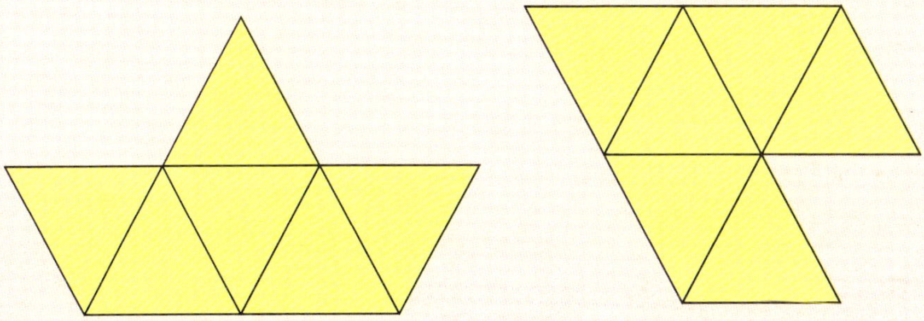

Make and draw **three** other shapes with 6 triangles.

Weather machine

Do Workbook page 22.

Angles are measured in **degrees**. **One degree** is a very small turn and can be written as **1°**.

This angle is one degree.

A right angle is 90°.

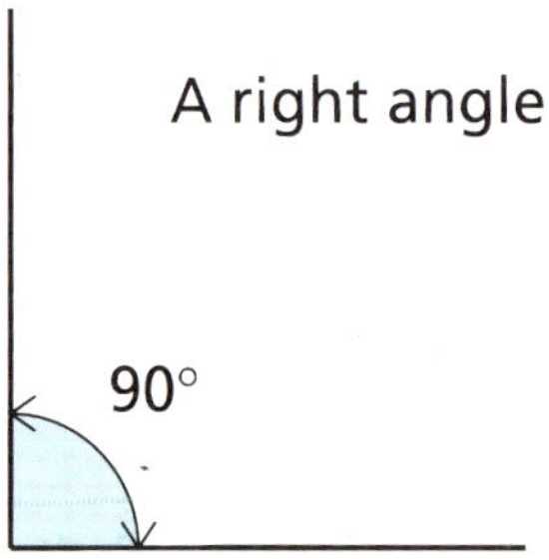

This angle shows a turn of 45°.

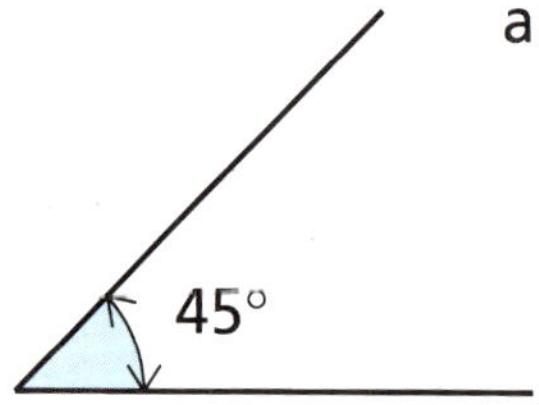

1 Copy and complete this table.

Right angles	$\frac{1}{2}$	1	$1\frac{1}{2}$	2	$2\frac{1}{2}$	3	$3\frac{1}{2}$	4
Degrees	45°	90°						

2 Start at *Fair* **each time.** What weather is shown when you turn the red pointer

(a) 90° clockwise

(b) 90° anti-clockwise

(c) 45° clockwise

(d) 180° anti-clockwise

(e) 225° clockwise?

3 Through how many degrees and in which direction does the pointer turn when it goes from

(a) Fair to Breezy

(b) Breezy to Sunny

(c) Sunny to Snowy

(d) Snowy to Stormy

(e) Stormy to Rainy

(f) Rainy to Frosty

(g) Frosty to Cloudy

(h) Cloudy to Sunny?

Fishing fleet

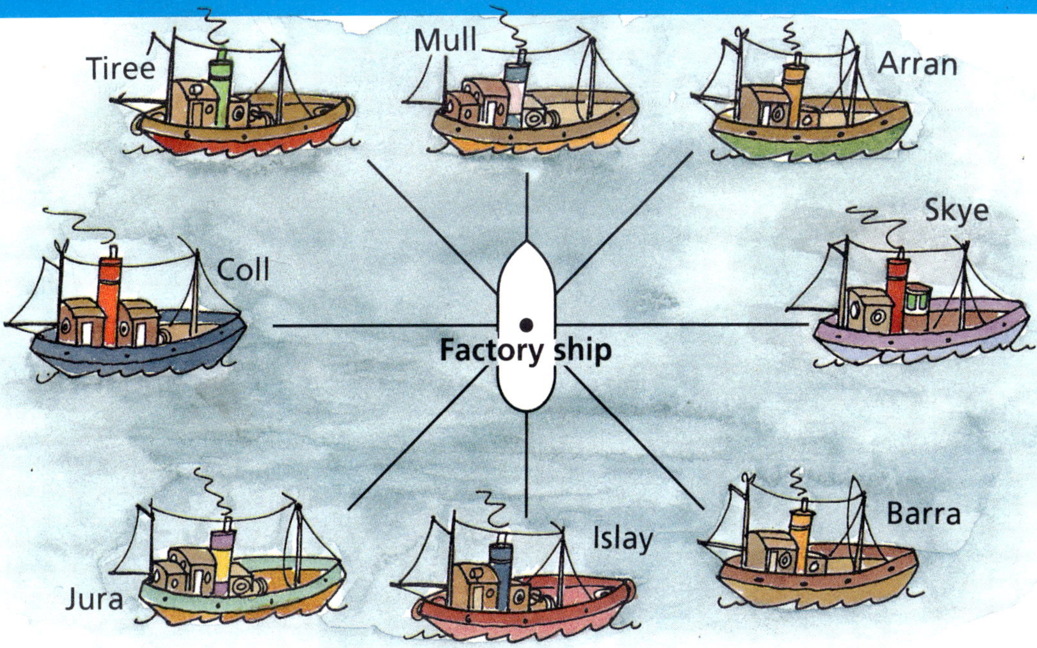

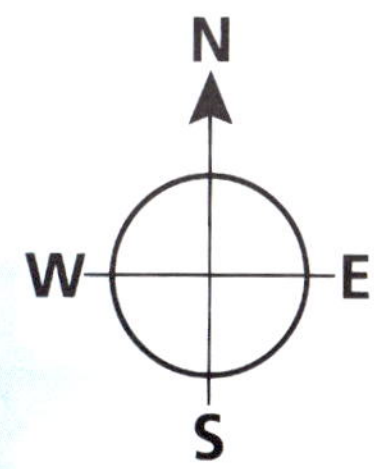

Hamish is on the factory ship in the middle of the fishing fleet.

1 Which boat does he see when he looks

(a) North **(b)** West **(c)** Northwest
(d) Southeast **(e)** Northeast **(f)** South?

2 In which direction is he facing when he turns from **North**

(a) 90° clockwise **(b)** 45° anti-clockwise
(c) 135° clockwise **(d)** 90° anti-clockwise
(e) 135° anti-clockwise **(f)** 180° clockwise?

3 Copy and complete the table.

Hamish faces	he turns through	he now faces
Skye	90° clockwise	
Arran	180° anti-clockwise	
Tiree	135° clockwise	
Jura	360° anti-clockwise	
Coll		Islay
Arran		Skye
Jura		Tiree
Barra		Mull
	135° anti-clockwise	Skye

Ask your teacher what to do next.

Lisa's robot

Lisa's robot understands commands like these:

FD 2 ⟶ move **2** places **forward**
BK 3 ⟶ move **3** places **back**
RT 90 ⟶ turn **90°** or **1 right angle** to the **right**
LT 90 ⟶ turn **90°** or **1 right angle** to the **left**.

Lisa gave the robot commands to write her name.

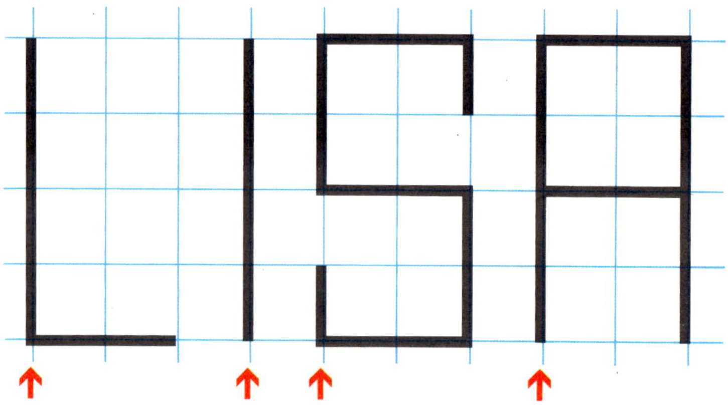

Lisa used these commands for the letter **L**.

FD 4, BK 4, RT 90, FD 2.

1 Write commands for the other letters. Start with the position and direction shown for each letter.

2 Lisa gave the robot commands to write her brother's name. Follow these commands on squared paper and write his name. Start facing this way ↑ each time.

First letter: FD 4, RT 90, FD 2, RT 90, FD 2, RT 90, FD 2.
Second letter: RT 90, FD 2, BK 2, LT 90, FD 2, RT 90, FD 2, BK 2, LT 90, FD 2, RT 90, FD 2.
Third letter: FD 4, LT 90, FD 1, BK 2.
Fourth letter: same as second letter.

Problem solving

3 Write the commands for Lisa's robot to draw this shape **without** going along any **line** more than once. Start where you wish.

Newspaper round

You need Workbook page 23.

Use these commands: **FD, BK, RT 90, LT 90.**

1 Write the commands for Pete's route from his house to the Newsagent's shop.

2 Follow these routes on the map. Where does each end?

(a) Start at Smallburn Inn:
FD 2, RT 90, FD 1, LT 90, FD 3, LT 90, FD 12.

(b) Start at Torwood Tower:
FD 6, LT 90, FD 5, LT 90, FD 2, RT 90,
FD 2, RT 90, FD 1, LT 90, FD 2.

3 It is possible to travel between 2 places on the map using only 1 command. Name the 2 places.

4 **(a)** Write commands for each of these routes. Use as few commands as possible.

- Pete's house to Hillend Farm
- Pete's house to Torwood Tower

(b) Which of your routes used fewer commands?

5 Pete starts **and** finishes his paper round at the Newsagent's. He visits each place marked on the map **except** his own house. Write the route for Pete's round using as few commands as possible.

6 These commands describe a route which **ends** at Torwood Tower. Where does this route start?
FD 2, LT 90, FD 5, LT 90, FD 4, RT 90, FD 6.

Problem solving

Ask your teacher what to do next.

Cora's computer

Cora likes playing games on her computer.

1 In this Space game what is at

(a) **D2** **(b)** **A3**
(c) **C3** **(d)** **A1**?

2 At what position is

(a) the flying saucer
(b) the satellite?

In this Driving game positions are given using **numbers only**.

- The police car is at position **2,4** (along 2, up 4).
- The petrol pump is at position **4,2** (along 4, up 2).

3 What is at

(a) 7,2 **(b)** 5,1 **(c)** 4,4 **(d)** 1,3 **(e)** 3,3?

4 At what position is the

(a) car **(b)** dog **(c)** lamp post **(d)** traffic warden?

Try these games from Cora's computer.

1 Secret messages

The code for CORA is

5,1	4,2	2,4	3,3
↓	↓	↓	↓
C	O	R	A

5	E	I	P	H	D
4	N	R	W	T	Y
3	K	V	A	U	L
2	M	S	X	O	J
1	B	G	Q	F	C
	1	2	3	4	5

(a) Find Cora's secret message:

3,4 1,5 5,3 5,3 | 5,5 4,2 1,4 1,5

5,4 4,2 4,3 | 3,3 2,4 1,5 | 2,5 1,4

4,4 4,5 1,5 | 4,5 3,3 5,3 5,3 | 4,2 4,1 | 4,1 3,3 1,2 1,5

(b) Write your own secret message to a friend.

2 Telepics

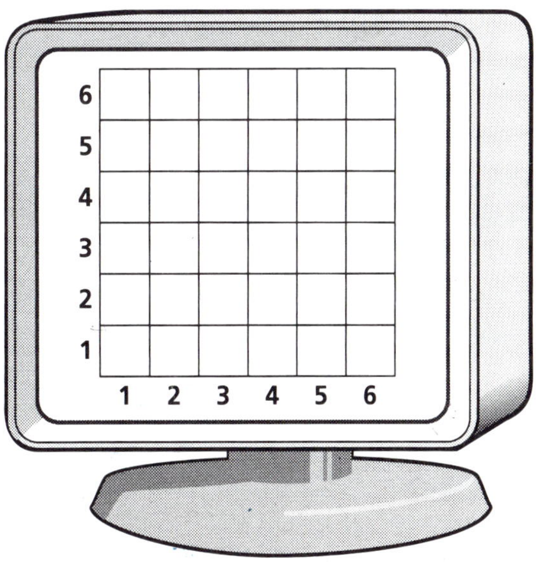

(a) Copy this screen grid on centimetre squared paper.

(b) Colour these positions red:
1,1 2,6 6,1 6,5 1,2 2,5
5,2 6,2 2,2 5,4 2,4 5,5

(c) Colour
- blue 3,3 4,3
- green 3,2 4,2
- yellow 3,4 4,4

(d) Draw eyes in the yellow positions and give your 'Telepic' a name.

3 Triples

A game for two.
Ask your teacher how to play.

Ask your teacher what to do next.

Circles

1 Use objects like these.
Draw round them to make circular patterns like these.

2 Draw and colour **circle** patterns of your own.

1 Work with a partner.

(a) Use this method to draw circles on a large sheet of paper or in the playground.

(b) Use the same method to draw patterns like these.

2 (a) Use a plastic strip with holes, pencil, paper and drawing pin to draw other circles.

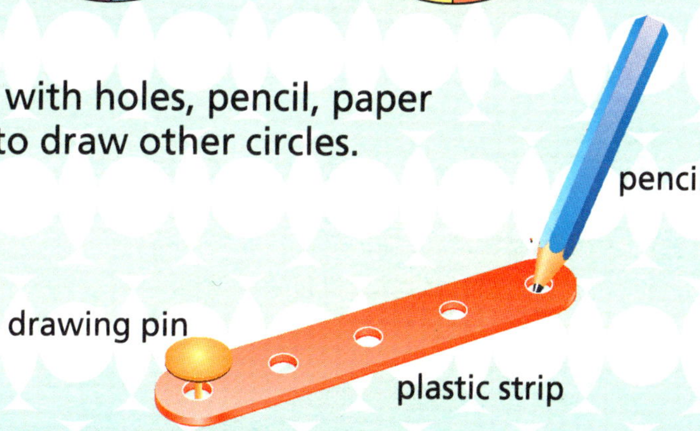

(b) Use the same method to draw a pattern.

Class 5 are finding out about the wood with the help of Dan, the Ranger. The red group are investigating where insects are found.

Insects found on one day this year

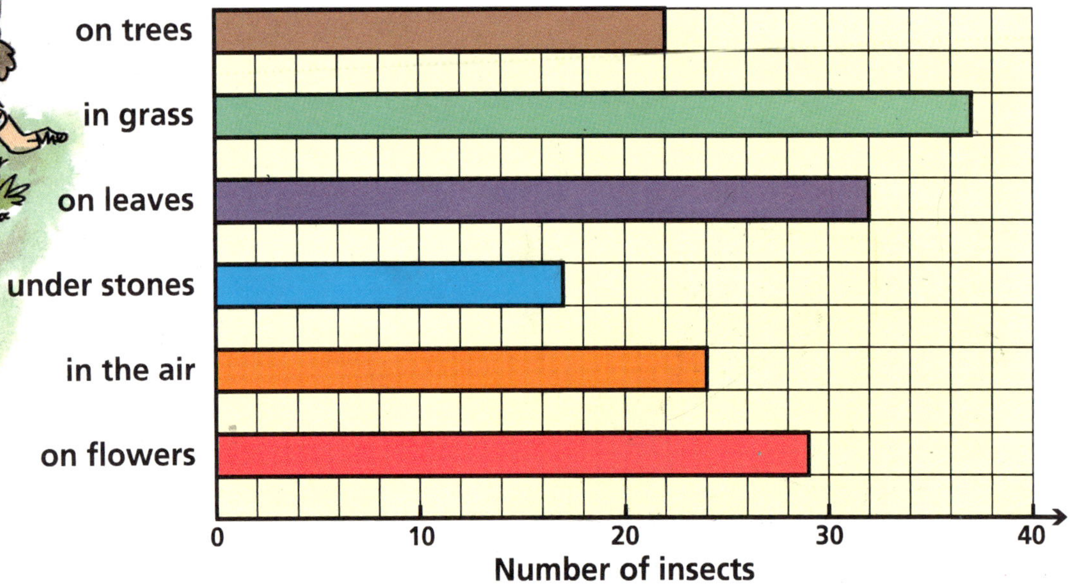

1 How many insects were found

(a) on leaves **(b)** under stones **(c)** on flowers?

2 How many **more** were found in the grass than

(a) under stones **(b)** in the air **(c)** on flowers?

3 What was the total number of insects found?

4 **(a)** Draw a bar graph using the information in this table.

(b) Look at the graphs for this year and last year. What has changed most? Why might this be?

Insects found last year

on trees	18
in grass	31
on leaves	27
under stones	8
in the air	13
on flowers	6

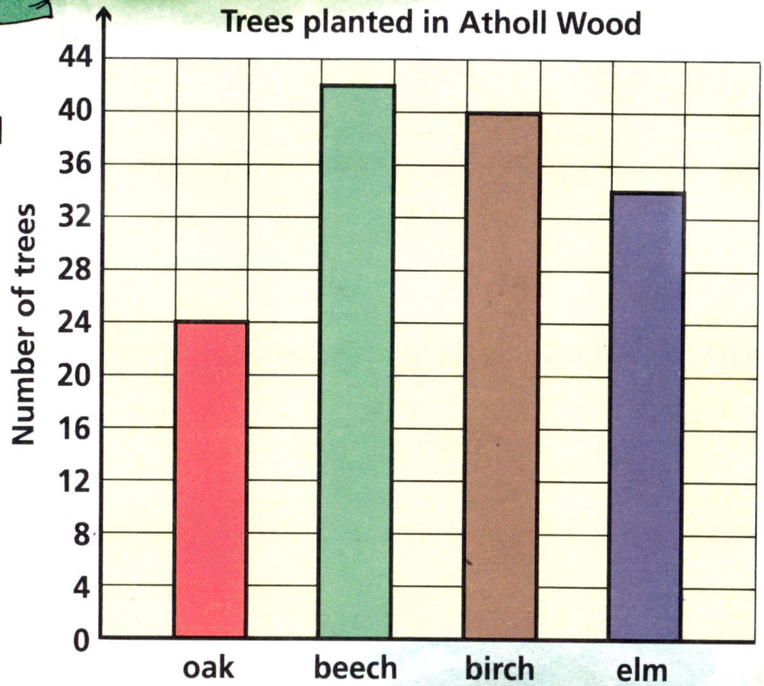

The green group planted trees in Atholl Wood.

1 How many of each type of tree did they plant?

2 What was the total number of trees planted?

3 The Ranger wants the group to plant more trees so that there will be the same number of each. How many of each tree should they plant?

The blue group keep a record of the number of finches at the bird tables.

Each  represents 10 finches.

 represents between 20 and 30 finches.

4 How many finches were seen between
 (a) 9 am and 11 am
 (b) 3 pm and 5 pm?

5 Between which times were there
 (a) fewer than 40
 (b) more than 50 finches?

Finches at the bird tables

6 When is the best time to see most finches?

Summer visitors

One day in March, Dan the Ranger made a count of birds which had arrived in Atholl Wood for the summer.

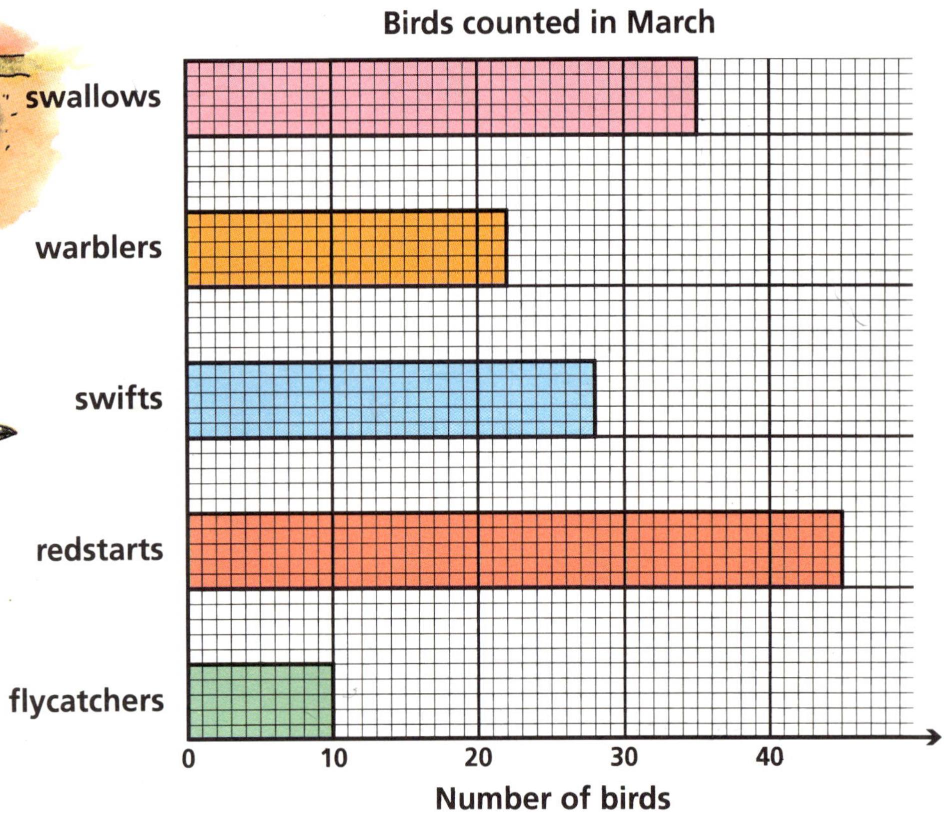

1 **(a)** How many of each type of bird were counted?

(b) What was the total number of birds?

2 One day in May, Class 5 made a count of the same birds.

Draw a graph, like the one above, to show the birds counted in May. Use the same scale.

Birds counted in May	
swallows	38
warblers	27
swifts	40
redstarts	45
flycatchers	21

3 **(a)** Which birds have increased in number, from March to May?

(b) Why do you think this happened?

(c) How many more birds altogether were counted in May than in March?

Every year birds arrive from different countries to spend the summer in Atholl Wood.

Birds from different countries

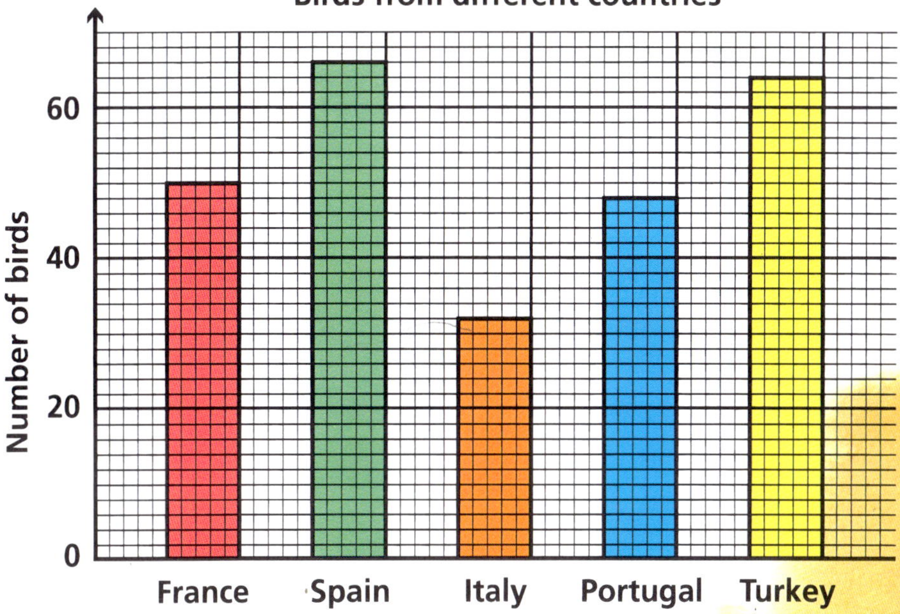

1 **(a)** How many birds came from each country?

(b) Find the total number of birds from the 5 countries.

(c) Is it true that more than half of these birds came from Spain and Portugal?

Six years ago, Dan ringed 100 young birds. Every year since, he has counted those that have returned to Atholl Wood.

2 Draw a graph to show the information in this table:

Ringed birds returning to Atholl Wood

Start	Year 1	Year 2	Year 3	Year 4	Year 5	Year 6
100	60	56	50	48	22	4

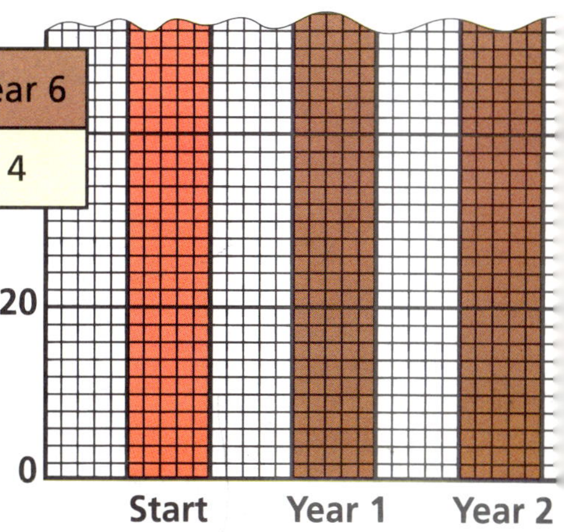

3 **(a)** How many ringed birds did not return in Year 1?

(b) Think of a reason for this.

(c) Why do you think so few returned in Years 5 and 6?

Animals in Atholl Wood

1 The blue group made a survey of animals in Mill Copse. They used tally marks grouped in fives (𝍸).

Animals in Mill Copse

Deer	𝍸 𝍸 |||	
Squirrels	𝍸 𝍸 𝍸 𝍸 𝍸 |||	
Rabbits	𝍸 𝍸 𝍸 𝍸 𝍸 𝍸 𝍸 𝍸 𝍸 𝍸 ||	

(a) How many of each animal did they count?

(b) How many animals did they see altogether?

2 The green group made a survey in Berry Glade.

Animals in Berry Glade

Deer	𝍸 |	
Squirrels	𝍸 𝍸 𝍸 𝍸 𝍸 𝍸 𝍸 ||||	
Rabbits	𝍸 𝍸 𝍸 𝍸 ||	

Altogether, how many fewer animals did they find in Berry Glade than in Mill Copse?

3 The green group made a survey on Fern Hill.

They counted
- 9 deer
- 8 rabbits for every 1 deer
- half as many squirrels as rabbits.

Copy and complete the table.

Animals in Atholl Wood

	Fern Hill	Berry Glade	Mill Copse	Total
Deer	9			
Squirrels				
Rabbits				
Total				

Go to Workbook page 34.

Would you touch. . . ?

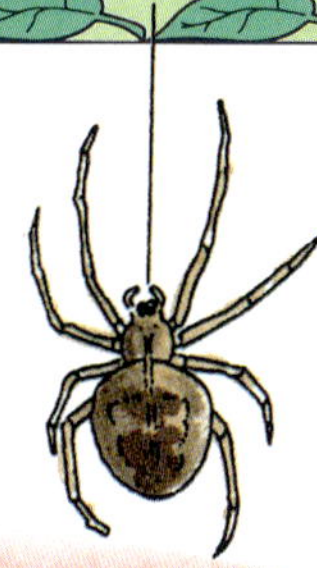

1 Use a tally chart like this to survey 60 children.

Would you touch a spider?

		Total
YES		
NO		

Would you hold a worm?

		Total
YES		
NO		

2 Would more than $\frac{1}{4}$ of the children

- touch a spider
- hold a worm?

3 **(a)** Do you think more adults than children would

- touch a spider
- hold a worm?

(b) Carry out a survey of 60 adults.

4 Copy and complete these tables.

spider	children	adults
YES		
NO		

worm	children	adults
YES		
NO		

5 **True or false?**

(a) More adults than children said they would

- hold a worm
- touch a spider.

(b) Less than $\frac{1}{2}$ of **all** those surveyed would touch a spider.

Go to Workbook page 36.

Yellow group's insect survey

Atholl Wood	6 July 6.00 am to 11.00 pm				WEEK 1
Insect	**number surveyed**	**colour**	**body length**	**food**	**can fly?**
ladybird 	48	red and black	$\frac{1}{2}$ cm	greenfly	yes
hover-fly 	44	black and yellow	$2\frac{1}{2}$ cm	nectar	yes
lacewing 	40	green	1 cm	greenfly	yes
violet ground beetle 	28	dark purple	3 cm	slugs	no
cardinal beetle 	16	orange and black	$1\frac{1}{2}$ cm	wood	yes

1 Where and when did the survey take place?

2 For how many hours did it last?

3 What was the total number of insects surveyed?

4 Is it true that

(a) more than half the insects surveyed had 2 colours

(b) the ladybirds made up more than $\frac{1}{4}$ of the total?

5 Use the chart to identify these insects.

Problem solving

6 Write clues that Dan could give so that Laura's answer is correct.

These are the yellow group's survey results for two kinds of insect in **Weeks 2 and 3**.

Week 2

ladybirds 卌 卌 卌 卌 卌 卌 卌 卌 卌 |

hover-flies 卌 卌 卌 卌 卌 卌 卌 卌 卌 ||||

Week 3

ladybirds 卌 卌 卌 卌 卌 卌 卌 卌 卌 卌 |

hover-flies 卌 卌 卌 卌 卌 卌 卌 卌 |||

1 Copy and complete this table.

Insects	Week 1	Week 2	Week 3	Total
ladybirds	48			
hover-flies	44			
Total	92			

2 **(a)** How many ladybirds altogether were surveyed in the three weeks?

(b) How many more hover-flies were surveyed in **Week 2** than in **Week 1**?

(c) In which week was the greatest number of insects surveyed?

(d) In which weeks were more ladybirds than hover-flies surveyed?

3 Julie finds that Ross forgot to record 5 ladybirds in **Week 2**.

Change your table to include the 5 extra ladybirds. **Remember to change some of the totals as well!**

Ask your teacher what to do next.

Atholl Wood averages

The red group raised money for the Atholl Wood project.

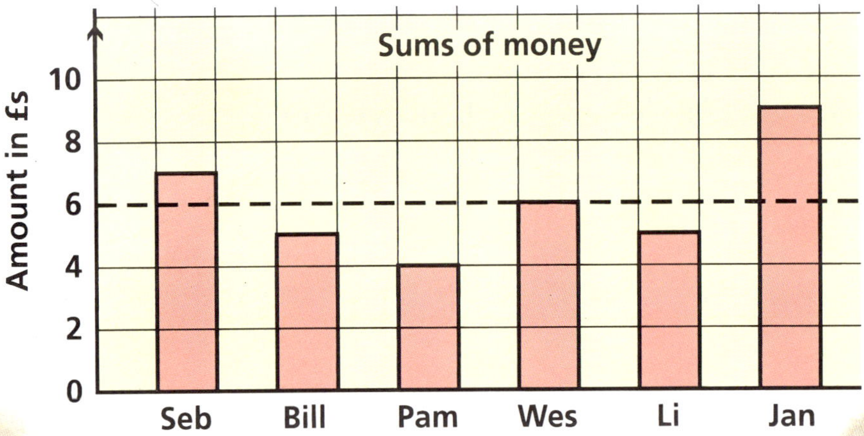

1 (a) How much did each child raise?

(b) What is the total amount of money raised?

(c) If each child had raised the same amount, how much would this have been?

(d) The dotted line on the graph represents this amount. Who collected exactly this amount?

(e) Name the children who raised

- more than this amount
- less than this amount.

At Atholl Wood, the green group spent time

sketching flowers	(F)
collecting leaves	(L)
counting birds	(B)
planting trees.	(T)

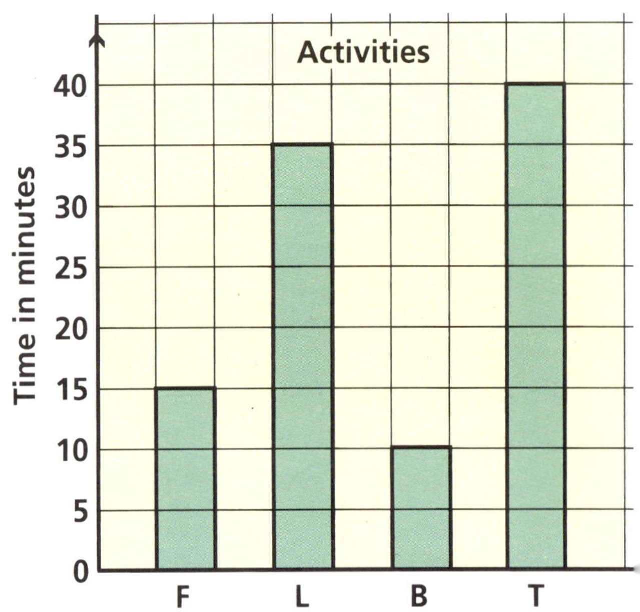

2 (a) How long was spent on each activity?

(b) If the **same time** had been spent on each activity, how long would this have been?

(c) Put a ruler across the graph to represent this length of time. Did any activity take this time?

(d) Which activities took

- more time than this
- less time than this?

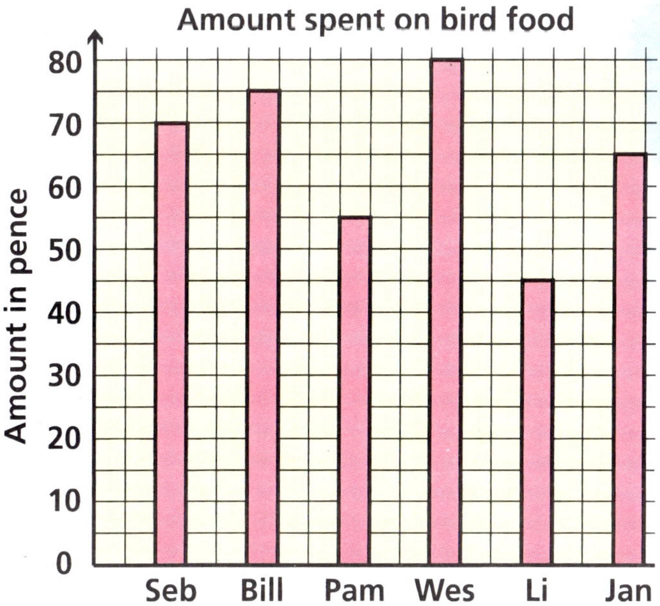

1 (a) How much did each child spend on bird food?

(b) What was the total amount spent?

(c) If each child had spent the **same** amount, what would this have been?

This amount is called the average or mean.

To find an average
- find the total
- divide by the number of items.

Money spent at the Visitors Centre

Seb	Bill	Pam	Wes	Li
95p	80p	50p	75p	60p

2 (a) Find the average amount spent.

(b) Who spent
- more than the average
- less than the average?

	Mon	Tue	Wed	Thu	Fri	Sat	Sun
Number of visitors	84	67	92	51	79	121	143

3 (a) Find the average number of visitors per day.

(b) On which days was the number of visitors above average?

Investigations

Last year, the Ranger measured these pine saplings.

Sapling	A	B	C	D	E	F
Height	77 cm	97 cm	69 cm	103 cm	78 cm	62 cm

1 **(a)** Find the average height of the saplings.

(b) Which saplings were
- above this average height
- below this average height?

The green group measured the same saplings **this year**.

Sapling	A	B	C	D	E	F
Height	120 cm	126 cm	114 cm	136 cm	108 cm	98 cm

2 **(a)** Find the average height of the saplings now.

(b) Which saplings are
- above this average height
- below this average height?

3 What do you notice about the growth of sapling **A**?

4 Investigate and write about averages in your class and school.

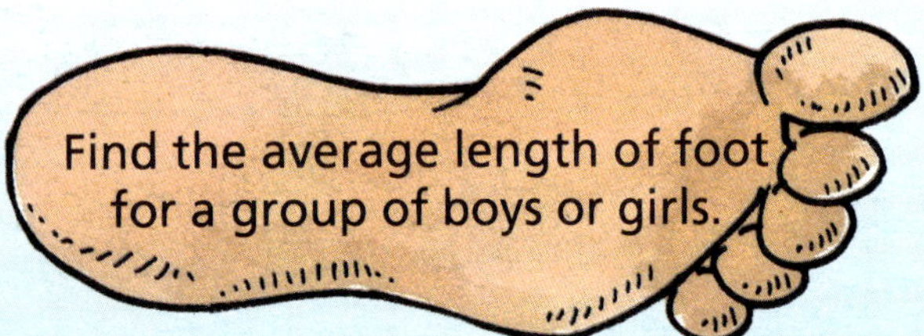

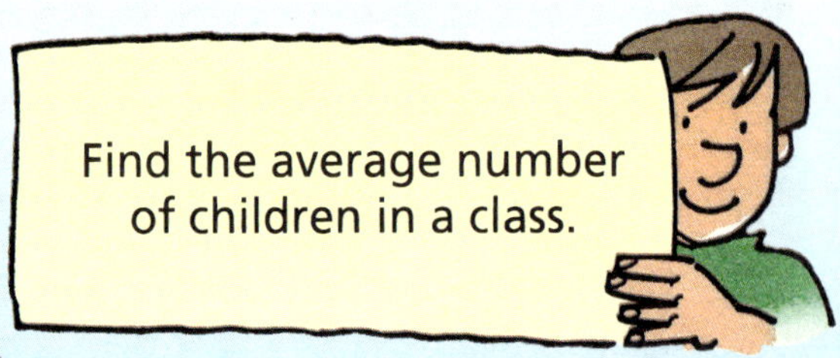

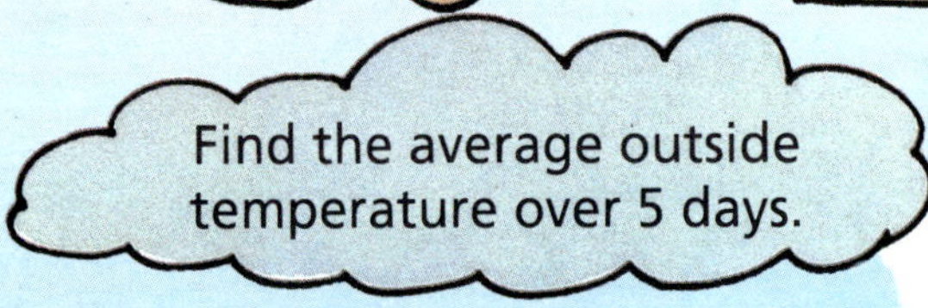

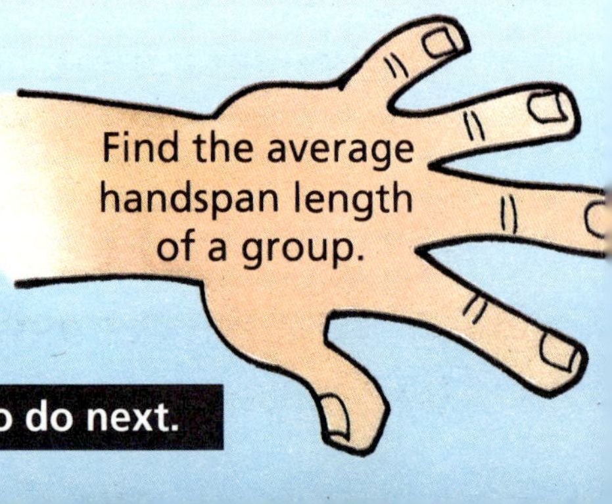

Find the average number of letters in first names for your class.

Ask your teacher what to do next.

Fair game?

1 Dan takes one badge from each card, without looking.
Which colour is **more likely** to be picked?

(a)

(b)

(c) Two brown badges are removed from card (**b**).
Is the chance of picking a green badge now

- less than even
- even
- more than even?

2 Read the rules for the Atholl Wood game.

- Put 1 yellow and 5 red cubes in a bag.
- Put a counter on the Visitors Centre.
- Shake the bag. Without looking, pick one cube. Move your counter along a path of the same colour as the cube.
- Put the cube back. Pick and move once more.

(a) **Estimate** at which place you are
- **most likely** to finish
- **least likely** to finish.

(b) Try the game 10 times. Record your results.

(c) Where is the most/least likely place to finish?

(d) Suggest changes to give you a better chance of winning.

Butterflies

1 The yellow group drew this scale for events during a walk in Atholl Wood.
Describe how likely they thought each event was.

2 **(a)** Draw and label a scale like this.

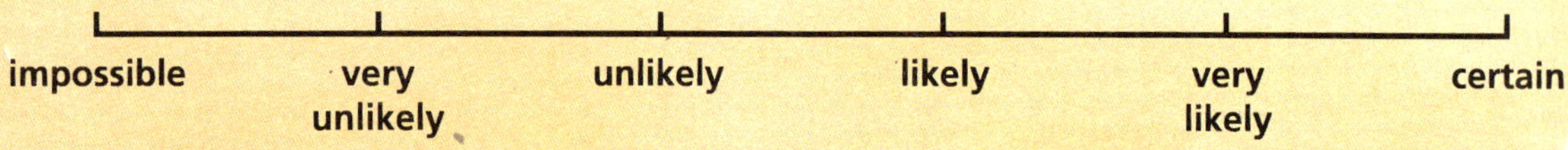

(b) Use the scale to show how likely you think these events are **for you** going home from school.

- see a train
- get wet
- start running
- spend some money
- talk to a friend
- use a pedestrian crossing

(c) Discuss your answers.

Problem solving

3 The graph shows when three types of adult butterfly are found in Atholl Wood.

Butterflies in Atholl Wood

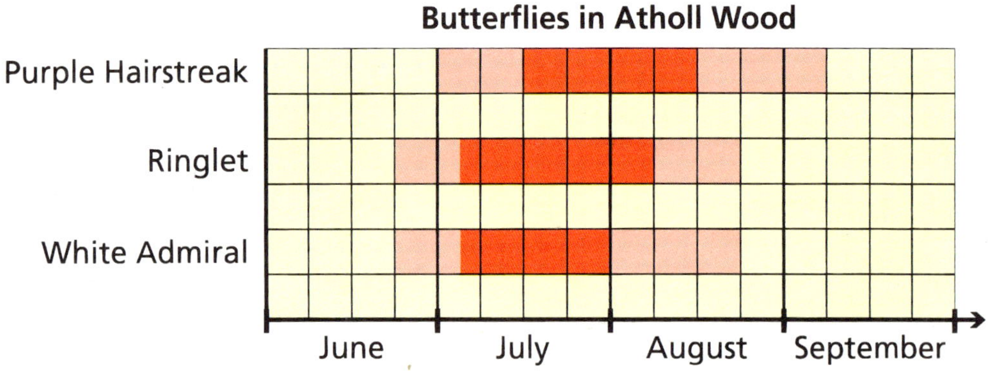

How likely do you think it is that each type will be seen
(a) in the last week of July
(b) in the first week of August
(c) in the last week of June?

Ask your teacher what to do next.

Shapes within shapes

You need dotty paper.

This shape has been divided and coloured to show 3 **identical** rectangles.

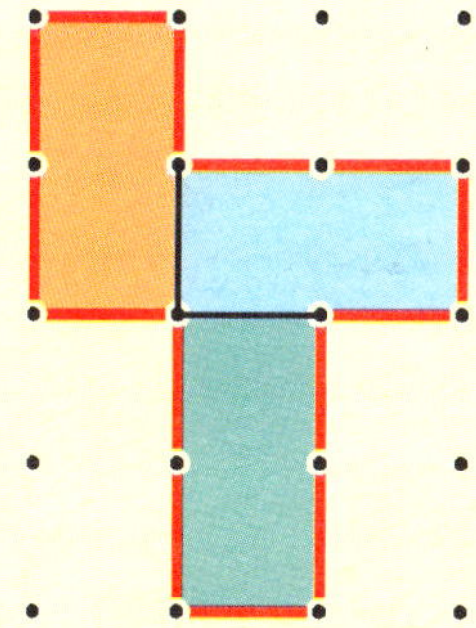

1 Copy, divide and colour to show

(a) 4 identical rectangles

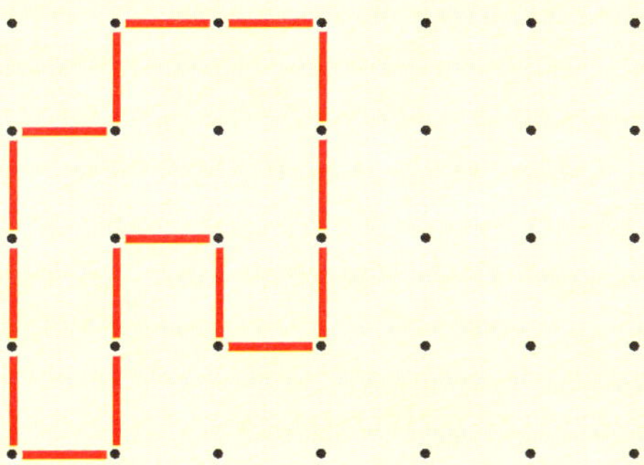

(b) 5 identical rectangles

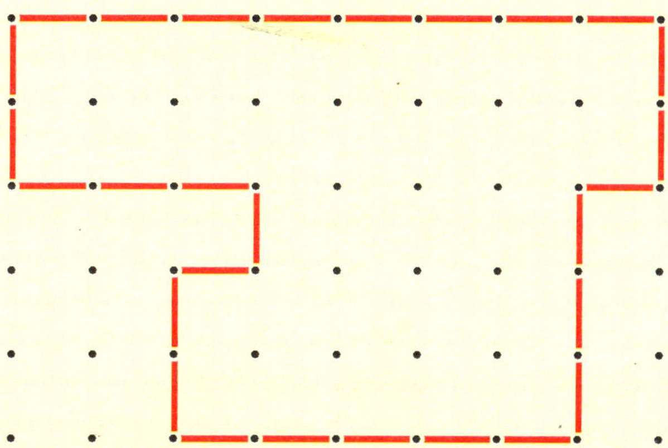

(c) 4 identical triangles

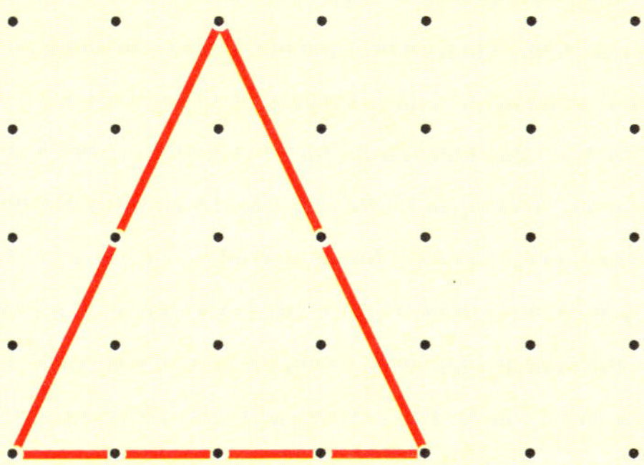

(d) 6 identical triangles.

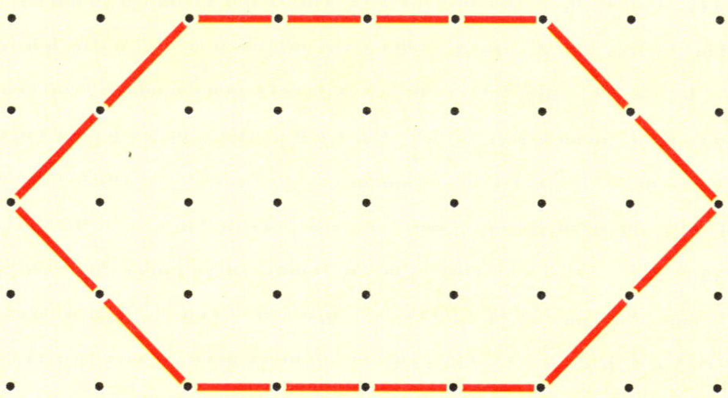

2 Find **two** ways to divide this shape into

(a) 4 identical triangles

(b) 8 identical triangles.

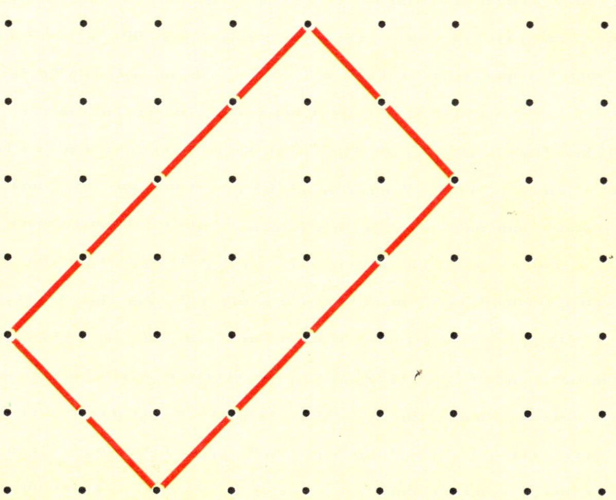

125 Recycling

Other activity: graphs

Paul and Jan collected cans for recycling.

Paul drew this graph.

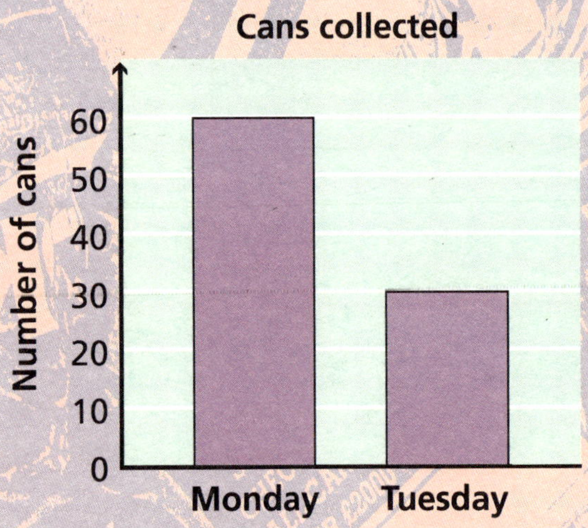

Jan drew this graph.

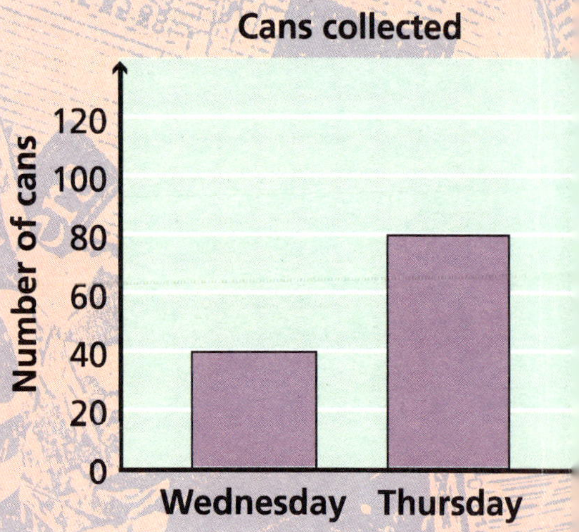

1 (a) Is what Paul says correct?

(b) Draw **one** graph to show this information for all four days.

(c) Which were the best and worst days for collecting cans?

(d) What is it about the first two graphs that caused Paul's mistake?

2 Jan drew this graph to show how many papers were collected on two different days.

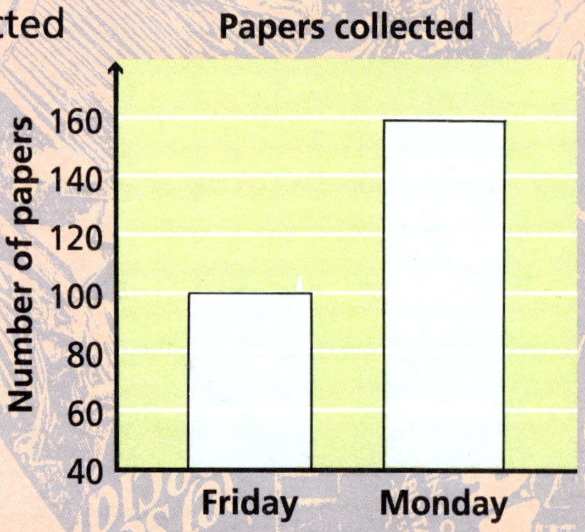

(a) Is what Jan says correct?

(b) Draw a new graph. Start the number axis with **0**.

(c) What is it about the first graph that caused Jan's mistake?